"I am fascinated and intrigued by Julia Gordon-Bramer's wildly and dizzyingly original readings of Sylvia Plath's poems. Not only does she make me realize that I need to go back and read the poems again, she comes pretty close to convincing me that I have really never read them at all."

—Troy Jollimore, National Book Critics Circle Award for Poetry, Guggenheim Fellowship for Creative Arts Recipient

"Julia Gordon-Bramer's *Decoding Sylvia Plath's 'Daddy'* presents the iconic poet in full three-dimensional view. Or six-dimensional, if you prefer. This Sylvia Plath is far more than the depressive, suicidal drama queen and father-hater depicted in easier accounts of the poet's life. Plath emerges as the genius's genius. Ms. Bramer's tone adds enjoyment to her already rigorous and penetrating work."

—Robert Nazarene, founding editor, *The American Journal of Poetry*

"In *Decoding 'Daddy': Discover the Layers of Meaning Beyond the Brute*, Gordon-Bramer deals the reader a full house out of the tarot deck, the occult, the Qabalah, mythology, and alchemy that leads both casual readers and critics alike to wonder just what they have overlooked amidst the general cacophony surrounding the circumstances of Plath's personal life and relationships. As the Grecian Fates once embroidered people's lives from the threads of fate, Gordon-Bramer weaves her mysticism into a cogent tapestry of deeper, transcendent interpretation of Plath's work and meaning in modern letters.

—Prof. Robert Masterson, CUNY-BMCC, New York City

"The guide takes a friendly, conversational approach so students feel empowered instead of overwhelmed. Its focus on topics not covered by other guides enables students to make original, insightful commentary, making it a worthwhile investment for those seeking deeper insight into Plath's work."

—Cathleen Allyn Conway, editor, *Plath Profiles: An Interdisciplinary Journal for Plath Studies*

Decoding Sylvia Plath's "Daddy"

DISCOVER THE LAYERS OF MEANING
BEYOND THE BRUTE

INCLUDES A GUIDE FOR STUDENTS AND TEACHERS

Julia Gordon-Bramer

St. Louis, Missouri

Copyright © 2017 by Julia Gordon-Bramer

All rights reserved. No part of this publication may be reproduced, distributed or transmitted in any form or by any means, including photocopying, recording, or other electronic or mechanical methods, without the prior written permission of the publisher, except in the case of brief quotations embodied in critical reviews and certain other noncommercial uses permitted by copyright law. For permission requests, write to the publisher, addressed "Attention: Permissions Coordinator," at the address below:

Magi Press
331 N. New Ballas Road #410176
Saint Louis, Missouri 63141-9998 USA
(314) 529-3904

Ordering Information:
Quantity sales. Special discounts are available on quantity purchases by corporations, associations, and others. For details, contact the "Special Sales Department" at the address above.

Publisher's Cataloging-In-Publication Data
(Prepared by The Donohue Group, Inc.)

Names: Gordon-Bramer, Julia
Title: Decoding Sylvia Plath's "Daddy": discover the layers of meaning beyond the brute / by Julia Gordon-Bramer
Description: St. Louis, MO : Magi Press, a division of *Night Times*, LLC, [2017] | Series: Decoding Sylvia Plath's-- ; [1] | "Includes a Guide for Students and Teachers." | Includes bibliographical references.
Identifiers: ISBN 978-0-9991860-0-8 | ISBN 0-9991860-0-0 | ISBN 978-0-9991860-1-5 (ebook)
Subjects: LCSH: Plath, Sylvia. Poems--Criticism, Textual. | Fathers in literature.
Classification: LCC PS3566.L27 D343 2017 (print) | LCC PS3566.L27 (ebook) | DDC 811/.54--dc23

Cover Design by Traci Moore
Editing by BookEval.com

Acknowledgements

Thanks to everyone involved in creating this book, but most especially to Tom Bramer, my husband and best friend, who keeps everything in balance and has supported me from the get-go with my Plath obsession. I am forever indebted and really do not think I could have taken on this overwhelming endeavor without your steadfast presence. Thanks to my two incredible sons, Sam and Ross Gordon, of whom I could not be more proud. A shout-out goes to Cathy Bowman, Catherine Rankovic, and Melanie Smith: fellow Plath scholars, fine teachers, gifted poets, and great friends. Big gratitude to my first readers and blurb-writers Cat Conway, Troy Jollimore, Robert Masterson, and Robert Nazarene. Appreciation (always) to the Indiana University-Bloomington's Lilly Library and staff, who are always welcoming and helpful when I go digging into the wonderful Sylvia Plath archives, what I like to call "my happy place." Kudos to Traci Moore for the cover design. There are too many dear friends in my orbit to name, but I'll try to catch the nearest ones: Matina Balint, Shaheera Bhutto, Aparna Brickner, Darren Drury, Gene Ferrier, Matthew Freeman, Zulfikar Ghose, Tim Jordan, Stella O'Brien, Nicholas Petricca, Patti Petricca, Tom Reynolds, Michelle Rubin, Judy Ryan, Theresa (Ti) Sumner, and Sharon Tutko. Thanks to all my old Night Times friends and the St. Louis music community, who will see this new book is closer in voice and spirit to our great old zine (I will get that memoir published in 2018!); the St. Louis literary community who have always stood by me, and who I've neglected since I committed so much of my life to Sylvia Plath and stopped going out so much (there is only so much time…). Love to my family and my in-laws, who, after almost twenty years of marriage feels like I've grown up with you all too; and to new family Rosie Moore, Carolyn Richardson, and of course to my delightful and perfect nephew and niece, Jack Alexander and Emma June. Love to my Maryland friends forever; to my Wisdom Group (Judith, Judy, Ann, Catherine and Sharon), who keep me sane each Thursday morning; to

Beth Mead, Director of Lindenwood University's Creative Writing Program; and my devoted Plath class students (especially Caleb Alexander, Erika Alexander, Deb Atkinson, Michelene Bolan, Troy Casa, Samantha Chasse, Tovah DiPrinzio, Marin-da Dennis, David Gilmore, Amanda Hull, Jeni Lozauskas, Melanie Medved, Dina Mozingo, Wanda Mozingo, Kevin Smanik, Theresa (Ti) Sumner, Tiffani Valez, and Lynette Van Hise); my many tarot clients who long ago crossed over into friends. Finally, 2016-17 has been a big year of loss of Daddies: Frank William Svolba, Dale Drury, Ben Lanterman, and Joseph Petricca; and in loving memory of my dear friend since third grade, Michele Cole Kubas. I will see you on the other side. I am truly honored to have known you all.

Contents

What You Should Know Going In 3

About the Poem "Daddy" 7

First Mirror: Tarot and Qabalah 11

A Little About Qabalah 23

Second Mirror: Alchemy 31

Third Mirror: Mythology 37

Fourth Mirror: History and World Events 43

Fifth Mirror: Astrology and Astronomy 61

Sixth Mirror: The Arts and Humanities 65

Decoding Sylvia Plath's "Daddy" in the Classroom 73

Bibliography 91

For

Frank William Svolba

~all is forgiven.

Decoding Sylvia Plath's "Daddy"

The world is full of magic things,

patiently waiting for our senses to grow sharper.

—W.B. Yeats

CHAPTER ONE

What You Should Know Going In

Imagine if you had the ability to write a tight set of words that speak to your audience on multiple levels, resonating deep into belief systems, culture, tradition, and also reflecting what's going on around you. The kind of writing you *feel* more than consciously understand. The kind of writing with rhythm and meter that gets stuck in your head like a hit record. That's the spell of Sylvia Plath.

Do you want to understand poetry? I mean, *really* understand poetry, what it can do, and understand what makes a poem great? Do you want to understand Sylvia Plath? Do you want to understand what the word *mysticism* means, and how it affects your mind when you read literature by its practitioners, falling under its spell? You will shortly.

You are about to learn how to decode Sylvia Plath's poem "Daddy," from *Ariel: The Restored Edition* (2004, Harper Perennial Modern Classics), pages 74-76. "Daddy" might be the best-known and most-studied of Plath's poetic works. If you're a new reader of Plath, you've probably heard the basic bio: Sylvia Plath is a world-famous American-born poet who made her name in the late 1950s and early 60s (but became most famous posthumously). She might, unfortunately, be best-known for her drama: her tough marriage to poet Ted Hughes, and her infamous suicide. Because of this story, much of the world has interpreted Plath's work through a limited, autobiographical view, describing it as "confessional," "angry," "depressive," and sometimes also "feminist" literature.

Sylvia Plath's poetry is powerful. For the last fifty-plus years, she has had more than fans; Plath has *followers*: rabid, possessed, devoted readers who feel a kinship with her. Sometimes it's a kinship based on feminism, sometimes on depression, victimization, or her confessional spirit. These are all part of that famous biography. Sometimes one's connection to Plath's work can't be explained. I'm not going to tell you that those autobiographical elements in Plath's work aren't there. But reading Plath strictly this way is like describing her only as "a woman" and her poem "Daddy" as just "a poem." That's unbelievably limiting. I know you can do better than that.

This book is a guide to understanding Plath's "Daddy" through the *Fixed Stars Govern a Life: Decoding Sylvia Plath* system, by myself, Julia Gordon-Bramer. *Fixed Stars Govern a Life: Decoding Sylvia Plath,* Volume One (referred to as *FSGL*) was first published in 2014 by Stephen F. Austin State University Press. Over the next few years I will be reissuing an expanded and revised book on each poem I first decoded in Volume One, as well as releasing the never-before-seen *FSGL* interpretations for the poems that would be considered Volume Two. All poems will be published in small individual books like this one, available in ebook and paperback format through Magi Press. These small books allow me to have a bit more freedom and fun with the poems. I'm dropping the MLA format and the boring academic tone, starting here. This is a book for everyone because Plath is for everyone.

For more than a decade, I have been exploring Plath's work through an interpretation of tarot and mysticism—in which Plath and her husband had an intense interest and regular practice. When you see what I've found, you will be astounded. I've written a ton on my system elsewhere, so I won't repeat myself here, except to say that Plath's *Ariel* corresponds perfectly to the Qabalah Tree of Life, on which the tarot is based.

What does this mean and why should you care? Well, if you learn just the simplest facts about Qabalah and tarot, which I'll give you shortly, you will soon see that those who read Plath as strict autobiography have been reading her wrong for more than fifty years! It's a bold statement, I know. But just read on and see for yourself. It's my goal to show you that Plath's work is a lot more than just depressive reflections, confessional autobiography, and wishes for suicide. As you pull apart her poems with me, you will know this too. And you'll understand that the mass resistance to seeing Plath in this light must have more to do with career egos, repressed discomfort about spirituality, and fear of rocking the status quo. Facts are facts, and it doesn't take a brain surgeon, or even an alchemist, to connect these dots.

If you picked this book up with a preconceived notion of who Plath was and what her work was about, I intend to stun you and give you a whole new perspective. If you never knew much about Sylvia Plath, you will soon know more than most scholars today, and after a few *Decoding* books, you might begin to see mystical patterns in other artists' works too. This is life-changing stuff. Spread the word!

For more details on my decoding process, please read the introduction to *FSGL*, which can be found at no cost to you at https://lindenwood.academia.edu/JuliaGordonBramer.

Please note: Because of copyright restrictions, the poem "Daddy" is not reprinted here. Partial quotes and references are made as permitted.

CHAPTER TWO

About the Poem "Daddy"

Wait, isn't this poem about her father?

As you know, most readers immediately associate the Daddy figure in this poem with Plath's father, Otto Emil Plath, who died when she was eight years old. Plath's mother suggested traits of her grandfather are in there too. Close readers will add in Plath's husband, Ted Hughes, whom she had just separated from at the time. These men are in there, to be sure. We see the early death, the German-Polish-Austrian family backgrounds of her parents, and the (nearly) seven-year marriage to Ted Hughes. *Of course* there is *some* autobiography. But there's so much more.

When talking to the BBC in December 1962, Sylvia Plath was rather cagey in her introductions to the *Ariel* poems, of which "Daddy" is one. She presented her poems almost as stories with characters, distancing her autobiography. In her notes prefacing the poems, found on pages 195-197 of *Ariel: The Restored Edition*, Plath told the BBC that her poem "Daddy" was:

> "...spoken by a girl with an Electra complex. Her father died while she thought he was God. Her case is complicated by the fact that her father was also a Nazi and her mother very possibly part Jewish. In the daughter the two strains marry and paralyze each other—she has to act out the awful little allegory once over before she is free of it."

While there are definite similarities to Plath's own life experience, her words to the BBC are greatly exaggerated. There is no evidence that her father, a German-born immigrant to America, was ever a Nazi, or even a racist. Her mother, Aurelia Plath, was not known to be part-Jewish, although Aurelia's long-suffering nature might have made Judaism a good metaphor to Plath. It is Plath's mention of the Electra complex and the therapy of acting out the allegory that reveals the real gist of "Daddy." The Electra complex was a term first coined by the father of psychoanalysis, Sigmund Freud. Plath read a lot of Freud, especially during and after her recovery from her suicide attempt in 1953.

We are so fascinated by and seek to understand Plath's work because it gets and holds our attention. It speaks to the spirit. Let me take you on a tour now of Plath's poem "Daddy," and the spell it has put upon us all. Like the work of Sigmund Freud, this book will help you to make the unconscious conscious. The mystic principles Plath used, or should I say *alchemized*, in the structure of her work will soon make perfect sense to you. By the end of this book, I promise you'll never see this poem, or Sylvia Plath, in the same light again.

> "Words were originally magic and to this day words have retained much of their ancient magical power. By words one person can make another blissfully happy or drive him to despair [...]. Words provoke effects and are in general the means of mutual influence."
> —Sigmund Freud, *Introductory Lectures on Psychoanalysis*, 1915

Discovering the Connections

You already know that Plath was a master of creating flow from one poem to the next in her collection *Ariel*. Do you know how she did it? Whether it was intentional or not, many words, images, and themes pour over from one poem into the next. This connectedness undoubtedly contributes to a subconscious unification of themes and flow of information to keep the reader spellbound beyond the power of the rhythms and symbolism. Psychologist Carl Jung coined the term *synchronicity* to describe what he called *the acausal connecting principle*. It is a meaningful connection between inner and outer events which defy explanation as cause and effect. It is a glimpse into the underlying order of the universe. In Qabalah and much of mysticism, everything is connected.

The *Ariel* poem preceding "Daddy" is "The Rival." Both of these poems share the following words: *white, beautiful, woman, marble, you, looking/look*. The connecting *ideas* between "Daddy" and "The Rival" might be the most interesting. Consider the two poems' related subjects of Africa and (presumed black) villagers dancing. We see both a mausoleum and marble. We see abasing subjects and standing at a blackboard. There are stone and a statue; dying, and forms of the words *die* and *kill, loving* and *love, thinking* and to *think, looking for* and *eyes, nervous* and *scared*.

Interesting, isn't it? And it continues: Plath's "Daddy" and its following poem, "You're," share the connecting words of *common, back/backed, foot/feet*. The connecting ideas are *travel,* the almost-anagram of *do not do* and *dodo's mode*, and *I could hardly speak* and *mute*.

Ariel was first published in a reordered version edited by Ted Hughes after Plath's death. The loss of Plath's intended order meant that the intended connections and synchronicity of the book's original design went unnoticed until after *Ariel: The Restored Edition, a*

Facsimile of Plath's Manuscript, Reinstating Her Original Selection and Arrangement, was published in 2004.

There is some back and forth as to whether events of intuition, precognition, or clairvoyance can be called *synchronicity*, but we know from their writings and journals that Plath and Hughes both considered Plath to be highly psychic too. Some scientists say that synchronistic theory is grounded in quantum physics, fractal geometry, and chaos theory. Physicists show that when two photons are divided, no matter how far the distance, an injury or modification to one affects the other simultaneously. At deep levels, everything is caught and united within a web of information that transcends time and space. Is synchronicity just a happy coincidence? Plath did it in her *Ariel* collection forty times, organized in a specific mystical order (the Tree of Life). Plath's work will teach you to see this world in a way you never have before.

Before you get too hung up on the fact that you don't know tarot, or mythology, or alchemy, or whatever, to properly understand for yourself all of the mysticism I'm about to present, relax. I'm giving you the high-level overviews in plain language. This stuff is easily verifiable through any Google search. Check it out yourself; you don't have to take my word for it.

CHAPTER THREE

First Mirror: Tarot and Qabalah

Where "Daddy" Sits in the Minor Arcana

Much about Sylvia Plath's work has yet to be fully understood. This book is a beginning, and it all starts with Tarot and Qabalah. Where Plath's *Ariel* poems sit in their original order, as Plath intended, determines where they fit on the Qabalah Tree of Life. And the meaning of that place, or *station*, unlocks the meaning of the poem.

Plath's powerful poem "Daddy" is the 34th in the *Ariel* collection. It is aligned with the rank of the queens in the tarot's minor arcana (to learn more about the tarot and its major and minor arcanas, see the introduction of *Fixed Stars Govern a Life: Decoding Sylvia Plath*, Volume (*FSGL*). "Daddy" begins in the emotional place of a little girl's fear and weakness, and it ends in a woman's fierce aggression.

You will see in the *FSGL* introduction that every poem in Plath's *Ariel* aligns with a tarot card, thereby revealing each poem's separate and complementary layers of meaning, all part of the same mystical pie, like Freud's different levels of consciousness that make up a single individual.

You just read a quotation two pages ago by Freud, who considered words to be the first magic. Freud, and other psychotherapists since, relied heavily on words, verbal and written, for hypnosis in therapy. Hypnosis is a big part of this literary spell-casting. Ted Hughes practiced hypnotism and regularly hypnotized Plath to ease her menstrual cramps and to overcome bouts of creative anxiety or writer's block. Hypnosis is a relaxed, unfocused level of consciousness that we all enter spontaneously and often, opening us to influence and command. The words used in hypnosis guide us toward feeling, and they speak to our cultures, our personal histories, and the things that make us individuals. Hypnosis relies on rhythms and repetition. For hundreds of years, poets and writers have seen this as a huge opportunity for the power of the written word. Poems may be interpreted as incantations, and Ted Hughes literally called them such, intending them as spells. Stories can also be seen as spells.

"In the beginning was the word."

Many biblical scholars define God as The Word, and Sylvia Plath's Unitarian Universalist upbringing would have been open to this thinking. Hughes and Plath identified their literary idols (Dante, Shakespeare, Chaucer, Milton, Blake, Yeats, Eliot, and others) as all having used modes of mysticism to influence readers through their writing. There are scores of observations of Ted Hughes' alchemy and spellcasting in his poetry, but for some reason no one thought to look at this in Plath's work. Until now.

So, what do words and hypnosis have to do with tarot? And how does this transport us "back, back, back" to "Daddy"?

Tarot accesses that intuitive/hypnotic place in our consciousness, and the cards' interpretations are usually communicated through words. Tarot is structured upon the Qabalah, and both tarot and Qabalah rely on intuition and acceptance of the occult—something a traditional, scientific worldview does not accept. But Plath did. The evidence is everywhere, beginning with Plath's spiritually open-minded church, and her childhood journals even include mention of her Sunday school homework studying the zodiac and Greek myths. Still in grade school, she drew pictures of Greek goddesses, carved an alchemical caduceus from wood, and much more. Plath's education was broad, and her spirituality was certainly not traditional; it was one based on energies and mystical influences versus a traditional Christian, authoritarian, egotistical, paternalistic God in the sky.

You're going to read the word *Qabalah* a lot in this book. You probably heard about it when Madonna started wearing the red string around her wrist. But you don't have to wear anything, or even believe in anything, to understand what Plath has done as I explain it here. All you need to know is that Qabalah is the mother of all occult sciences upon which most occult practices are modeled, and so they correspond to each other and have many similarities.

Qabalah's reach is universal: It covers the tangible world, seen in world events, history, the arts, and also the spiritual realm. You'll see what I mean in a minute. Qabalah explains why the figures in astrology and the astral bodies in astronomy are named after mythological characters. It's the reason alchemy was the first science, and why so much in alchemy and chemistry overlaps, and so on. Tarot is an excellent method of learning Qabalah, and the student can identify a tarot card for every station and path of the Qabalah's Tree of Life. On each card can be found corresponding astrology, mythology, numerology, alchemy, and more. There are even references to a mystical chess game, which we'll also talk about later. Tarot represents all the tools for making magic. Think of the tarot as Qabalah flash cards.

Ever since we separated church and state (a really good thing), science has unfortunately refused to accept anything at all to do with that which is not evidence-based, and so the proverbial baby gets thrown out with the bathwater. This rejection of the spiritual actually gives anyone working with arts or emotion an edge, if not respect. Freud said it like this:

> "Your earlier education has given a particular direction to your thinking, which leads far away from psychoanalysis. You have been trained to find an anatomical basis for the functions of the organism and their disorders, to explain them chemically and physically and to view them biologically. But no portion of your interest has been directed to psychical life, in which, after all, the achievement of this marvelously complex organism reaches its peak. For that reason psychological modes of thought have remained foreign to you. You have grown accustomed to regarding them with suspicion, to denying them the attribute of being scientific, and to handing them over to laymen, poets, natural philosophers and mystics."
> —Sigmund Freud

In a more recent book, *The Power of Impossible Thinking* by Wind and Cook (2006, FT Press), it is explained that our pre-determined mindsets, our "mental models," create what we see and limit our outcomes. You will be astonished at what no one has seen for over half a century which was directly in front of them. We might consider it a poetic sleight of hand!

The goal of qabalists is to reach the point of not just experiencing or meeting God but destroying the physical self *to become God*—at one with the source. Defining God is up to you. Generally speaking, it's considered to be a place of wisdom, purity and new life. And so, like the other literary masters steeped in occult tradition whom they admired, Plath and Hughes appear to have sought to master these energies within their work, thus casting a quiet spell upon their readers. It seems to have worked.

As seen across the bounty of her writing, and in some of *Fixed Stars Govern a Life*'s other interpretations of Plath's poems, Plath identified with the underdogs, such as Jews and the gypsies[1], both wandering peoples without a home over much of history. Both the Jews and gypsies were demonized in the Crusades and during World War II and sent to Hitler's concentration camps. Plath, we know, had an eye for metaphor and grabbed onto this loaded Jew-gypsy imagery, most especially in her poem "Daddy."

Legend had it that gypsies carried the tarot across the world as they traveled and were exiled from one place to the next during the Crusades. These are the Romany people, who were given the name *gypsy* as they were incorrectly and perhaps romantically identified as coming from Egypt, much as Native North Americans were called *Indians* due to Columbus' confused navigation.

The "Egyptian gypsy" myth has clung to the tarot by association with these people, and so the lore is that the tarot embodies secrets of ancient Egyptian cults, *The Book of the Dead*, Hermes Trismegistus, Thoth, Rosicrucianism, and more. This book isn't about focusing on these, except to say that Western schools of occult studies, such as Rosicrucianism and the Hermetic Order of the Golden Dawn, incorporated signs, symbols, and meaning from these teachings into tarot decks made after 1900. You will see occasional references to them in *Fixed Stars Govern a Life*.

If you have read Plath's journals and letters, you already know that she adored the fictional gypsy Heathcliff in Emily Brontë's *Wuthering Heights*, comparing him to her own Ted Hughes. The idea of the gypsy was reflected in her ancestry, with her Austrian-Hungarian-Polish roots, as well as the gypsy's lure of mysticism.

Plath received a book on tarot with a tarot deck from Hughes on her 23rd birthday. The book was *The Painted Caravan: a penetration into the secrets of the tarot cards* (1954, L.J.C. Boucher, The Hague), written by Basil Ivan Rákóczi, a self-proclaimed Romany gypsy who

---

[1] The term "gypsy" is now and has been considered a racial slur for more than 30 years at the time of this writing. In Plath's day it was viewed differently. We will use the term here as it references Plath's writing and also atrocities to the Romany people in World War II. This word is written in lowercase throughout this book as it was never an ethnic group's proper name.

both proudly illuminates and exaggerates the mystical gypsy myth and legends in his book. Plath identifies this spiritual path in "Daddy":

> "With my gypsy ancestress and my weird luck / And my Taroc pack and my Taroc pack."

Taroc, the Italian name for the tarot, is a game using tarot cards, also called *Tarocchi*. Plath has many journal entries mentioning playing Taroc with her family as a girl. In *The Painted Caravan*, Rákóczi speaks of his people avoiding judgment by the church-government by hiding the secrets of the occult in the deck of cards and presenting it as a game. In this same way, Plath presents tarot in her poem, connecting it to gypsies and "weird luck." Yet the reader knows there is no pleasure, and this is no card game she is playing, in the poem "Daddy." This is full-on mysticism.

On page 70 of *The Painted Caravan*, Rákóczi writes the following about the minor ("lesser") arcana:

> "Gypsy Masters are fond of allotting the names of Egyptian, Greek and Roman divinities, or of their secret Gods to many of the Lesser Arcana, and often add to these Astrological or Zodiac Signs and some special quality or virtue. Furthermore, they are in the habit of giving the cards the names of famous historical or fictional characters, which may be called their Key Types or Guardians."

Bottom line: This is what Sylvia Plath has done with each poem in *Ariel*. Plath's poems are the flash cards for the flash cards.

Obviously, falling under the spell of Plath's work will not cause you any harm. No hypnosis can force people to do something they are unwilling to do. I'm mentioning it so that you become aware of the mystical processes at work in Plath's—and many other writers'—literature.

In my first book, *Fixed Stars Govern a Life: Decoding Sylvia Plath*, I present each of Plath's *Ariel* poems and where it hangs upon the Qabalah's Tree of Life. The Tree of Life is a map of the soul's journey from birth to death, corresponding to the major arcana and then to the minor arcana ranks, and finally ending with the four suits (represented by Plath's "bee poems"): Cups, Swords, Pentacles, and Wands. Beyond that order of the poems, each *Ariel* poem has what I call a *mirror* with a corresponding qabalistic subject, as Rákóczi described. I identify them this way: Tarot and Qabalah; Alchemy; Mythology; History and the World; Astrology and Astronomy; and the Arts and Humanities. Each poem has one metaphorical foot in emotion and spirit, and the other in history and things of this world.

In "Daddy," Sylvia Plath is ready to assume her spiritual power and to become one with God, her God-self, which as you learned is the goal of the qabalist. With its paternalistic title and themes of war and suffering, Plath's "Daddy" is the surprise poem to represent the tarot deck's four queens. I'll say it again, because I know you have been pre-programmed to think "Daddy" is only about masculinity: Plath's poem "Daddy" connects with all four queens on the Qabalah Tree of Life. And boy, are they mad. This poem's negative tone explains why the queens' meanings are mostly in reverse (upside-down, as they face the tarot reader), focusing on these personalities' most negative properties. In the tarot, fathers are often represented by the Kings rank, and of course, the queens are married to these men. Right off the bat, Plath's "not do" of the first line counters the *I do* vow of marriage.

In *Ariel Ascending*, edited by Paul Alexander, Ted Hughes wrote that while he used mysticism to pursue new forms of creativity, Plath sought occult means to try to reach her dead father. And we once saw Plath trying to communicate with her dead father in her long poem, included in Ted Hughes "Notes: 1957" of *The Collected Poems*, "Dialogue Over a Ouija Board." It is this *recovery* that we see mentioned in "Daddy." However, in "Daddy," Plath seems to have a moment of clarity. She realizes that every bad man, every reversed king, duplicates the dominance of a father over his daughter when the relationship is abusive. Every bad father, then, becomes a Nazi to Plath. This abuse also mirrors the Father-God relationship. Some of this you're smart enough to have already picked up on your own, even if you know nothing about tarot. But let's learn a little bit about the history of the queens:

Meeting the Queens in "Daddy"

As in a pack of playing cards, there are four suits in the tarot, each with "court cards": King, Queen, Knight, and Page. Take a look at pictures of these tarot cards online if you would like to understand more about their visual imagery. The tarot deck Plath owned in 1956 was most likely the Rider-Waite tarot deck, as few others were in mass production at that time. Today, the modern Universal Waite tarot deck is very similar. All aspects of these four queens star in Plath's poem "Daddy." You'll soon see how they open up the poem for us:

The Queen of Wands

You've probably met some version of her before in your own life. The Queen of Wands, when the card appears reversed, represents an unstable and sometimes crazy, deceitful and vengeful woman. Her suit of Wands is about energy, enthusiasm, and life, but in her reversed nature—look out! She is destructive, dark feminine energy. Because this queen is often a mother and, in her upright position, loves animals and children, Plath's nursery-rhyme qualities chosen for the poem "Daddy" fit her well. Wands are attached to the element of Fire and the fire signs in the zodiac, and in Greek mythology this queen is represented by Penelope or Atalanta.

The reversed Queen of Wands's tone is at the heart of "Daddy"—she is done with paternalism. Plath cuts all ties to the father figure starting with the first lines of the poem.

The Queen of Cups

Here comes the drama queen! The Queen of Cups reversed signifies instability, bipolarity, and tumultuous, painful love, all fitting the ambiguity and love-hate feeling of the poem "Daddy." The suit of Cups is about emotion, creativity, and physical and mental health and this queen is attached to the element of Water. The Queen of Cups reversed has been betrayed and is seen as unwell and/or a victim. She corresponds in Greek mythology to Helen of Troy.

The tarot picture of her match, the King of Cups, is well-described in "Daddy": "And your neat moustache / And your Aryan eye, bright blue." Because the Queen of Cups reversed is also unstable, there is a curious attraction to this bad king whose call still pulls at her. We see it later illustrated in the line: "Panzer-man, panzer-man, o You—" Panzer is a German word meaning armor.

Throughout the poem "Daddy" there is ambiguity: reverence and love for this Daddy-man who has brought so much anger and pain. This tumultuous, masochistic kind of love represents both the King and Queen of Cups in their emotional roller coasters. She represents the water signs of Pisces, Cancer, and Scorpio, the last of those being Plath's zodiacal sun sign. One can't help but think that Plath probably identified with this queen.

The Queen of Pentacles

There is always the one who is out for herself: The Queen of Pentacles reversed lives within her ego, and her suit of Pentacles focuses on materialism and the things of the world. She is Omphale in Greek mythology. Pentacles are attached to the element of earth and the earth signs of the zodiac. We see the Queen of Pentacles' point of view beginning with the third line: "In which I have lived like a foot / For thirty years, poor and white." The Queen of Pentacles reversed is overly concerned with possessions and power and fights to express herself against dominating forces. Like a foot, she is stuck at the root chakra issue of survival, the lowest point. Feet and roots are both clearly within the poem "Daddy."

The Queen of Swords

And here's the baddest of the villainesses, the one we love to hate: The Queen of Swords reversed is not to be messed with! She represents a lonely, hot-tempered woman with an unhappy emotional life. Toughest of the queens, she's motivated by burning jealousy and spite.

If you know your Greek mythology, she is the murderous Clytemnestra, the toughest of the queens. Swords are attached to thought, action, and the element of air and air signs in the zodiac. Reversed, the vicious Queen of Swords may also represent a divorcee, a widow, or a woman who has given up on men, sex, and love. Swords represent thought, speech, and a sharp tongue. This queen's speech is halted because of anger: "I never could talk to you. / The tongue stuck in my jaw" and "Ich, ich, ich, ich. / I could hardly speak." She does what she must to have her way: "Daddy, I have had to kill you."

Ach, du! Another Mystical Queen

In Plath's collection *Ariel*, elements of the game of chess appear in many poems. Reference to chess isn't entirely surprising, because authors such as Lewis Carroll have incorporated chess characters and strategy into their fiction, and many qabalists practice a variant of the game called Enochian Chess.

In both traditional and Enochian Chess, the queen is the strongest piece on the board, and in "Daddy" this chess piece is speaking to her king made of marble. If we read the poem through the lens of chess, in earlier games the narrator played a losing white side ("poor and white /Barely daring to breathe"). However, now, as the black queen, she is more aggressive. If she is captured, it is a battle and a prayer "to recover" her by getting a pawn to the opponent's line. The chess-piece king, of course, has a cross on his crown ("full of God"). The board game is "flat," and certainly chess is about the "wars, wars, wars" seen in this poem.

Opponents are mostly silent when playing chess, as in the fifth and sixth stanzas of "Daddy." In the eighth stanza, we see a fact about Plath's "Taroc pack," designed so its court cards match the personalities of chess pieces. The winner of a chess game becomes a "Fascist," adored for both his intellect and brutality, as in the tenth stanza. Finally, Plath knows that if she gets her opponent's king, she also beats her opponent ("If I've killed one man, I've killed two—"). As first seen in Plath's "Morning Song," which is the corresponding poem for the pawns in chess, each pawn is said to represent an ordinary citizen of a village and his trade ("And the villagers never liked you"). One knows that the game is over when the king cannot escape, seen in this poem's last few lines.

The "Daddy" of this poem is the king on his throne in a God-like sense. Both the King of Swords and the King of Pentacles's images in their tarot card pictures are what could be "Marble-heavy, a bag full of God, / Ghastly statue with one grey toe / Big as a Frisco seal" (although the King of Swords' toe is red). And wouldn't you know, both the King and Queen of Cups sit beside the green and blue ocean ("the freakish Atlantic / Where it pours bean green over blue").

But wait! There's a lot more.

CHAPTER FOUR

A Little About Qabalah

Why Would Plath Care?

I'm interrupting (already!) this mystical tour through the mirrors to give you just a smidgen of background. The occult sounds awfully creepy, doesn't it? We think of Halloween skeletons and witches, séances and contacting the dead. But it's not really about any of that. The word *occult* means *hidden*, and the thinking is that this is spiritual stuff hidden from the masses. It is clearly not for everyone.

As you read earlier, there is loads of documented evidence that Plath and Hughes dabbled in or regularly practiced astrology, hypnotism, used the Ouija board, crystal balls, tarot, and so on. From the earliest times, and especially since the Crusades, the occult and its practitioners have gotten a bad rap from radical religious types and a lot of people who are afraid of what they don't know or what seems weird to them. Occult practices continued to be illegal in the United Kingdom until 1951, and the stigma remained long after.

Wonder why Plath kept so quiet about her occult endeavors? There are plenty of reasons: She had a history of mental illness and would have risked being called "crazy"; her serious career in a then-uptight and conservative academic world; her publishing pursuits in respected publications; and her young children whom she wanted to protect from gossip and harm.

The occult sciences, all under the umbrella of Qabalah, seek to bring an individual from a base level of existence to self-actualization and becoming one with God. To the occult-haters: That's not so bad, is it? It's actually quite positive if you're into expanding your talents and optimizing your potential. The Qabalah's Tree of Life is a kind of roadmap to self-actualization and owning your God-power.

> "The tree of life and the tree of life"
> —Sylvia Plath, from "The Munich Mannequins"

You'll see me use the word *mirrors* a lot in *Fixed Stars Govern a Life*, in this book, and in other *Decoding* books. In *Kabbalah and Criticism*, author Harold Bloom claims the right-hand station of the kings to be called "father of fathers," comparing them to Freud's imago of the father. The matching queens on the opposite side of the tree are the mothers, representing intelligence and passive understanding. "Kabbalah is nothing if not sexist," Bloom writes. Plath certainly observed the same. Bloom says the stations are "sometimes imaged as a mirror, in which God enjoys contemplating himself." Think of the mirrors I present here as the kind you see when trying on clothes in a department store. It is the same body, the same story, told from different perspectives. That's what Plath has done in her *Ariel* poems.

Qabalah, while originally a form of Jewish mysticism, is not about traditional religious faith, of which Plath had little, but about spiritual power. Qabalah is not about worshipping God, but rather about dismantling the ego and becoming a part of God. It must have been the ultimate quandary for Sylvia Plath, who since she was a child had called herself "the girl who wanted to be God," and later journaled about her many struggles with her huge ego and ambitions.

There are many spellings of "Qabalah." Don't let this confuse you; it's all essentially the same thing:

Kabbalah - Jewish mystical origins
Cabbala – Judeo-Christian version
Qabalah - Hermetic version (from the Hermetic Order of the Golden Dawn, late 1800s-early 1900s)
Also spelled *Kabbala, Kabala, Cabbalah, Qabala,* and other ways, depending on the sect.

And so, to recap:

The Qabalah Tree of Life is the divine formation and order of all things as they relate to each other.

The tarot mirrors the Qabalah Tree of Life in its ordering and symbolism ("flash cards"). I consider the first mirror in Plath's poems to be Qabalah and tarot itself. Plath's poems directly reflect the associated card(s) and meanings.

Poets and writers have been structuring their work in the order of the Qabalah since Shakespeare and Dante.

Plath and Hughes knew this, and Hughes went so far as to dedicate sixteen years of his life to writing a single book about Shakespeare's use of *Cabala*, called *Shakespeare and the Goddess of Complete Being* (1992, Farrar, Straus and Giroux). It is so fat and intimidating, however, that it has driven most readers away.

Racism and Endogamy

Admit it: You've struggled with Plath's use of the notorious "n-word" in her title poem "Ariel," or her Jewish, Nazi, and Ku Klux Klan references seen in "Daddy" and other poems. If you've done a bit of digging, you know Plath wasn't a racist, because she gave money to anti-apartheid causes and had friends of color in college. So why would she say such things? Well, one of the reasons is that Qabalah and its progeny sometimes use a now politically-incorrect metaphor of *endogamy*, or marrying within one's tribe or clan to keep a bloodline pure.

The spiritual ideal of racial purity runs throughout "Daddy" in the guise of the Nazi metaphor. It begins with the "black shoe." This black shoe is especially interesting, as her father Otto Plath's immigration documents list him as a "bootmaker." The theme is carried on with the German "Ach, du"—translated as a surprisingly sympathetic "Alas, you" in English—and the reference to wartime:

> "In the German tongue, in the Polish town / Scraped flat by the roller / Of wars, wars, wars."

Poland's borders have changed many times, and the Polish towns of Grabow, Pozen, and Budzyń, all listed on Otto Plath's documents as his town of origin, changed hands from Prussian to German rule and therefore put Otto Plath on both sides of the war.

Clearly, race was an issue Plath wrestled with, having witnessed World War II and Holocaust atrocities as a child on the movie theater newsreels. Her birthday, October 27, 1932, even coincided with Germany's National Socialism takeover, a connection that she no doubt made.

Plath was an educated woman. She would have known better than to use the slang term "Polack" without a greater meaning. One begins to pick up on a superior narrator mindset from phrases such as "My Polack friend," a derogatory expression even for its time in the early 1960s. To say "Polack" instead of "Polish" or "Pole" is to also side with the offensive Nazi-Daddy in addition to being a victim to him. In "Daddy," Plath lies back upon the analyst's couch and surveys her own evil and worldly feelings of superiority. After all, Plath too had her prejudices—adopting derogatory stereotypes even against the Jews, as she turned coldly against Hughes's family during her divorce.

It is interesting to note that Aleister Crowley, one of the founders of the famous Hermetic Order of the Golden Dawn and originators of the modern tarot deck, was an accomplished writer and poet himself. However, Crowley's writing was full of racism. We do not know Plath's feelings about Crowley, although she probably knew of him through her husband. Despite the fact that Crowley had learned so much from Indian yoga, the Chinese I Ching, Jewish Kabbalah, and Goetia, he did not believe in mixing blood.

About Plath's "Jew" References

Got the basics down now? Understanding that little bit of background about tarot and Qabalah will make the rest a lot easier. You've maybe noted that in Plath poems, many of the dates and claims are exaggerated. Is this poetic license? *No.* It references Qabalah. Now that you know that much, Plath's Jewish references should make a lot more sense:

Qabalah, originally Kabbalah, is a form of ancient Jewish mysticism.

The Hebrew language is considered mystical in and of itself, with numerical values assigned to each letter. Jews and Kabbalists believe that the Hebrew language has a divine origin and supernatural power, and the letters illustrate the process of God creating the world.

The Qabalah's Tree of Life positions each of the 22 Hebrew letters on their stations and paths.

The tarot's major arcana has 22 cards, reflecting these Hebrew letters and Qabalah positions.

Plath matched the Jews with the gypsies in the poem "Daddy" as having a similar history of wandering, homelessness, and persecution.

The Jews and gypsies both practiced their forms of mysticism.

> "I began to talk like a Jew. / I think I may well be a Jew."
> —Sylvia Plath, from "Daddy"

Ich, Ich, Ich, I am I

In German, *Ich* means "I"—the self, which is incapable of expression in the presence of "Daddy." If one believes that the true self, the spirit, is a part of God (as mystics do), then the successive utterances of the divine name were said to produce the four worlds of the Qabalah: *Aziluth, Beriah, Yezirah,* and *Assiya*. In Genesis 1 of the Bible, God creates the world with words, and so language has the ultimate potential for creativity. Plath played around many times with repetitive utterances of the divine words of the Creator, "I am" and "I am I," across her poetry, prose, and fiction.

The Black Consciousness of Ego

Just as hubris is the downfall of man and gods in mythology, Qabalah teaches that the only real evil is the ego, the "black" consciousness. Qabalists believe our egos teach that we are evil, but the ego is the true devil ("You stand at the blackboard, daddy, / In the picture I have of you, / A cleft in your chin instead of your foot / But no less a devil for that, no not").

Everyone, not only you, has a hard time in growing and transitioning out of the world and into the spiritual: "Panzer-man, panzer-man, o You—" This is Plath's clinging attachment to things of the familiar world, even when they are cruel. When one understands being torn between fleshly and spiritual concerns, one can more easily understand the ambiguity, that love-hate feeling, throughout "Daddy." Plath, like all of us, had attachments to the ego and the earthly world. Her creativity was God-given and channeled, and yet worldly ego and a constant drive for success got in the way. Purity is tough. She was at battle with her own endogamy.

"An engine, an engine / Chuffing me off like a Jew. / A Jew to Dachau, Auschwitz, Belsen" returns us to the imagery from the *Ariel* poem representing the tarot deck's rank of fours, "Getting There." This line portrays the great train moving through the stages of spiritual life, with the ego threatening to level all creation to blackness. But the interpretation of "Getting There" is for another book.

On Being Thirty

Aside from Sylvia Plath being thirty herself at the time she wrote "Daddy," thirty is the age at which Jesus Christ was baptized and received the Holy Spirit, and thirty might also refer to the Trinity. If we do the math in "Daddy," Plath suggests that she is around thirty years old in stanzas twelve through fifteen of "Daddy." It's interesting to note that Plath called herself thirty years old in three other poems "The Colossus" (1959), "Tulips" (1961), and "Lady Lazarus," (1962). The number thirty obviously takes on a larger meaning for Plath, more than merely her physical lifespan.

In Qabalah, scripture says that one must be over the age of forty, and male, to practice this mysticism. The consequences for breaking these rules is madness. Plath's mention of her age and sex seem to flaunt the fact that she is disobeying God, as well as to reinforce the feminist undertones of "Daddy."

CHAPTER FIVE

Second Mirror: Alchemy

The Next Great Adventure

"After all, to the well-organised mind, death is but the next great adventure."
—J.K. Rowling, *Harry Potter and the Philosopher's Stone*

Remember Harry Potter's fantastic alchemy class in the Hogwarts School of Witchcraft and Wizardry? A dark gothic building housed a laboratory of robed teenagers, under the watchful gaze of Professor Nicolas Flamel. That's the book and movie image you probably have when you think of alchemy.

Like most of Plath's poems, "Daddy" is full of alchemical imagery—especially appropriate because Plath's father Otto was a Freemason, and Freemasons have historically been practitioners of alchemy. Freemasons are members of an international order for mutual help and brotherhood, holding secret rites and using secret signs. Alchemy uses a lot of weird language with sexual and even incestuous metaphors to symbolize unions, purity of bloodlines, and so on. Alchemy is about uniting one's opposing worldly and spiritual selves—the "double" of whom Plath wrote so often in poems and stories.

The blackness throughout "Daddy" represents the black alchemical phase, or *nigredo* process, in the chemistry lab. In the alchemist's quest for the philosopher's stone, also known as the *magnum opus*, or perfect work, he or she must burn away the impure matter. Alchemical texts compare this burning to a brutal, torturous practice. *Nigredo* correlates with the third station of the Qabalah, where the rank of the queens and the poem "Daddy" fall in Plath's *Ariel* sequence.

Next comes *ablution*, or the washing and whitening of the stone in mercurial waters. Not surprisingly, this white stone is symbolized as a queen, to be united with the Red King in the chemical wedding, to create the perfect work. Now comes the creepy part of alchemy: This joining is usually portrayed as an incestuous union, emphasizing the essential similarity of the substances. *Eeeeeeew*. Trust me, it's symbolic only and gets back to that endogamy idea. The spiritual purity, plus the physical and emotional work to create this union produces the hermaphrodite or homunculus, best known as the Philosopher's Stone. "Homunculus" shows up in Plath's poem "Cut," and she has written of this image elsewhere. *Nigredo* explains Plath's use of the N-word in her title poem, "Ariel."

A Dictionary of Alchemical Imagery cites:

> "The incestuous coniunctio is most frequently represented as the union of brother and sister, but it is also represented as the union of mother and son, father and daughter, and king and son."

So, yes, it's hard to take if you're looking at it literally. And it is also nodding toward that Electra complex Plath mentioned, as well as Freud, and the Rain Queen, and more you will read about shortly.

The Element of Lead

I can almost hear that gutsy-wonderful rock empress Tina Turner belting out your thoughts now: *What's lead got to do with it?*

Well, war depends on lead (bullets, machinery) and lead is the base metal representing the lowest point of humanity in alchemy. The rank of Queens in the tarot aligns with the planet Saturn and the element of lead, represented by the Roman god Saturn, and his harvest scythe. If you look up lead's history, its chemical symbol is *Pb,* from the Latin root word *plumbum,* meaning "waterworks." It is a reference from ancient times to when the metal was used in the construction of pipes, but also an apt metaphor for the "waterworks" colloquialism for tears. Plath's "Daddy" suggests both kinds of water. Although there are twenty-seven lead isotopes, few are considered stable, instability being another strong metaphor for the tarot's reversed queens.

When layers of gray graphite were first lifted from the earth in England in 1565, it was mistaken for lead ore. From that time on, it has been a common misconception to call the core of graphite pencils *lead.* Pencil lead takes on meaning a little bit later when in the Arts and Humanities mirror we discuss a beloved book from Plath's childhood, *The Silver Pencil.*

Alchemical Symbols

Always on the lookout for persecution from the church or theft of discoveries from competitors, those enchanted Alchemists of Olde chose to hide their secrets through symbols and metaphor:

> "I could hardly speak"

Alchemical language is full of sexual metaphor:

> "the language obscene"

Some of Plath's alchemical symbols in "Daddy" include: "black"; "white"; "grey"; sea water; inability to speak (alchemical secrets); difficulty in understanding alchemical language and sexual metaphor;

"snows" (another description for the whiteness of the queen); "pure"; separation ("Bit my pretty red heart in two"); "the sack" (the alchemical bed, or container); "glue" (the bond or medium of conjunction, compared in alchemy to sperm); "the rack" (chemistry lab equipment); "blood" (the mercurial red tincture or elixir); and the overall idea of torture and suffering, as it pertains to the black phase of alchemy.

Killing the Ego

Can there be a victory in destroying part of the self? In "Daddy," we see the line "I used to pray to recover you" with its wonderfully weird double possibility: Could Plath have meant to re-cover, as in to bury again? Did she strive to kill a God who was already dead to her?

Psychologist Carl Jung, a student of Sigmund Freud's, evolved the ideas of practical alchemy in the laboratory to his process of *individuation*, thus creating Jungian alchemy. Jung's 1944 book *Psychology and Alchemy* analyzed alchemical symbols and showed a direct relationship between the psychoanalytical process and alchemy. For Jung, the alchemical transformation of the impure soul (lead) to the perfected soul (gold), was a metaphor for his *individuation* process, what psychologist Abraham Maslow would equate to *self-actualization*.

In line with this thinking, Plath viewed herself as her own abuser, her own "Daddy," trying to kill the ego to become something greater. We see a similar theme in *Fixed Stars Govern a Life*'s analysis of "The Jailor," also in the *Ariel* collection. Plath and Hughes read a great deal of Jung, and Plath most definitely believed that she had to kill her ego to become something greater, to find her true self. "Abandon my ego," Plath directed herself in her journals. Her ego, however, might have died on its own during her worldly troubles:

"Daddy, I have tried to kill you. / You died before I had time"

Note the word "had" in the seventh line. Father-God (Chronos in mythology) owned all time, past, present, and future, but Plath wanted her place in it. Her new, spiritual self must possess time and not merely be a point within it. A super-interesting point to make right now is that Chronos is often confused with Cronus, the Titan king who killed his father.

CHAPTER SIX

Third Mirror: Mythology

Mythology: The First Psychology

If we spin the clock's hands backwards in time, mythology was the first psychology; it is stories that explain the whole of human experience. And like the mystics and major religions of the world which blame the ego for pain and the dark side, mythology shows the cause of the downfalls of gods and man to be *hubris*. These ancient mythologies are so scarily accurate that the forerunner of psychology in the western world, Sigmund Freud, named the human complexes after the mythological stories and characters of ancient Greece.

Robert Graves wrote much about the roles of the mythological queens in *The White Goddess: A Historical Grammar of Poetic Myth*, which Plath and Hughes considered to be an example of the power of myth in literature. These same queens are also prominently featured within the works of Shakespeare, perhaps the greatest writer in Plath's and Hughes's eyes. Graves saw the spirit of the White Goddess displayed in all of Shakespeare's queens: Lady Macbeth, Cleopatra, and the "damned witch Sycorax" from *The Tempest*. Graves noted that Sycorax's eyes were blue, and that "blue-eyed" in Elizabethan slang also meant "blue-rimmed with debauch," much like Plath's Nazi "Daddy" character.

Ted Hughes's university major was anthropology, and primitive cultures and religion interested him from a young age. Plath, meanwhile, was well-schooled in the ancient Greeks, Romans, Celts, and her heritage of Norse mythology. Another favorite book addressing mythology for Plath and Hughes was Sir James George Frazer's *The Golden Bough*.

The queens grouped together on the Qabalah Tree of Life are found at the third station, *Binah*. It is the point of understanding, and represented by the planet and god Saturn. Saturn, with his *leaden* scythe, is most often pictured as the harvester or Grim Reaper. He is not a nice guy, and he does not joke around.

If you've read any myths, you know that characters and details can vary while treating the same themes, depending on which author tells the story. Now that you've met the tarot's queens and know the meanings of the cards, it's time to know a bit more about the mythological personalities these queens portray. The names might vary now and then, but these mythological queens fit the tarot card queens' personalities to a tee:

Meet Clytemnestra

At the same time Plath wrote "Daddy," Ted Hughes had been working on a translation of the Greek play *Oresteia,* part of a trilogy by Aeschylus. In the play, Queen Clytemnestra plans to murder her king husband, Agamemnon, as revenge for the sacrifice of their daughter Iphigenia. Again, a Daddy must die, at the hands of a queen.

The queen's other daughter is Electra, who was in love with her father. Plath wrote about Electra in the earlier 1959 poem "Electra on Azalea Path," a poem about mourning at her father's grave. One of the themes throughout the trilogy is that all the bloodshed is committed against the family. Fittingly, for the ancient Greeks, the murdering of a family member is perceived as equal to the murder of the self.

In *Oresteia*, a servant witnesses familial horrors from the top of the roof, where he claims he has been crouching for "years," and "under the instruction of a man-hearted woman." She sounds very much like the Queen of Swords, in reverse, and also reminiscent of Plath's "Daddy." The servant promises to keep silent, saying "A huge ox has stepped onto my tongue," echoing Plath again with "Ich, ich, ich, ich. / I could hardly speak." Sometimes Clytemnestra is equated with Medea.

Meet Helen of Troy

Many scholars consider the tarot's Queen of Cups to represent the beautiful Helen of Troy, daughter of Zeus. Motivated by passion and emotion contradictory to logic, Helen offered favors of her love even to enemies of her homeland ("Panzer-man, panzer-man, o You—").

Plath wrote about Helen of Troy by name in her 1958 poem "Virgin in a Tree." Helen of Troy's ambivalence and confusion are all over the poem "Daddy."

Meet Penelope/Atalanta

The Queen of Wands, like the Queen of Swords, was unwanted by her father. The tarot's Queen of Wands can be equated with Penelope, the chaste and ever-waiting wife of Odysseus, the wandering hero who left her for twenty years ("I used to pray to recover you"). In Homer's *Odyssey*, Penelope's ill-tempered father flung her into the sea as an infant.

The Queen of Wands is also considered to be Atalanta, the daughter of King Iasus. According to Hesiod, King Iasus wanted a son. When he was disappointed by the birth of a girl, he left the baby Atalanta on a hillside to die from exposure. Atalanta, the huntress, took an oath of virginity and wanted nothing to do with men. Animals saved the babies in both tales.

Meet Omphale/Thetis/Medea

The tarot's Queen of Pentacles, Omphale, was the wealthy queen who purchased the untamed and brutal Heracles in an auction to become her slave and lover as well as a cohort in practical jokes on Pan, the Devil. In "Daddy" we see Heracles's brutality in the "brute/ Brute heart of a brute like you," as well as in Plath's mention of the devil.

Author/mythologist Robert Graves, whom Plath and Hughes read avidly and whom Hughes knew personally, compares the parricide of Britain's King Brutus (see this poem's History mirror) with the tale of Evander, who was kicked out of Italy's Arcadia because the sea-goddess Thetis made him kill his father. These myths take us back to Plath's second and third stanzas of "Daddy" again. The angry Thetis, who also killed her children and required that a child be sacrificed to her at every winter solstice, oversaw the matrilineal succession of priestess-queens who represented her. According to Graves, these consorts took turns reigning for seven years each—the same amount of time Plath points out in "Daddy." Graves goes on to explain that Thetis is one of the maiden daughters of mythology who was rescued from the sea-beast king/father Poseidon. Achilles was the only son whom Thetis allowed to survive, and his existence turned the triple-goddess-oriented matriarchal system into a patriarchal one. So now we've got a real mythological punch in Plath's final line of the poem:

> "Daddy, daddy, you bastard, I'm through."

Telamon's Off at the Root

Achilles/Talus is also known as Telamon (close in sound to Plath's "telephone"). The vengeful goddess Medea killed Telamon. Medea is the other name for that Queen of Swords we just met. One of the meanings of Telamon, from its "root" of Tla or Tal, is "he who dares to suffer"—something anyone with "a love of the rack and the screw" might enjoy. He also gave King Telephus a wound that would not heal.

From the same root sound is the Greek myth of Telemachus, the "fatherless boy" as Plath defined him in an annotation in her personal copy of *The Portable James Joyce*. He is the son of Odysseus and our Queen of Wands's Penelope. In the first four books of *The Odyssey* Telemachus wanders searching for news of his father.

By now, I'm sure you see mythology all over "Daddy"!

CHAPTER SEVEN

Fourth Mirror: History and World Events

Plath's Evocation of History in "Daddy"

One of the huge pieces of decoding Plath's work is seeing the effect history had on her poems. The current events of her day might have inspired her, but she always seemed to draw from the deep well of the past at the same time. As you learn what was going on around her, watch how Plath's genius mind spun it back in history and also related it to her mythological and tarot themes. Plath considered herself to be an avid history buff and very political. She wrote newspaper and magazine editorials and letters to the editor about the subjects she was passionate about, such as ending the nuclear arms race.

In her copy of *The Portable James Joyce*, Plath underlined and starred this comment from the editorial introduction:

"he evoked the past to illuminate the present."

This idea was most definitely her intention with writing as well. Also in this book she underlined passages about Jung's "rational unconscious," collective myth, and the editor's statement

"Joyce has managed, by invoking an ancient myth, to conjure up a modern one."

Current events greatly affected Plath's poetry. She wrote "Daddy" on October 12, 1962. Ten days earlier Heinrich Deubel, Nazi soldier and commandant of Dachau concentration camp, died of natural causes in Bavaria. No charges were ever brought against him. The trial of SS Lieutenant-Colonel Adolf Eichmann, responsible for the deaths of thousands of Jews and gypsies, had gone on for much of the previous year and Eichmann was executed by hanging in June 1962. In the days building up to Plath's writing "Daddy," a host of "Daddy"-sounding events took place: the Sino-Indian war began; the Cuban Missile Crisis heated up; U.S. troops began to die in Vietnam; the remains of a medieval cog ship were found in Bremen, Germany; seven children were accidentally killed in a military parade in Szczecin, Poland; and twenty-eight people were killed and sixty-two injured in a train collision in Warsaw, Poland. These then-current events certainly dance around the periphery and mood of "Daddy," even if Plath didn't speak about them directly.

Britain's Brute, Brutus

Boom! Here's someone Plath *did* speak about directly. Before now, no scholar seems to have picked up on "the brute / Brute heart of a brute like you" as a nod to Brutus of Troy, who lived around 1150 B.C.E., about one thousand years before the Roman invasion and following the destruction of the city of Troy. Brutus sailed from Greece with the Trojans he had freed to—you guessed it, the Atlantic—to fight giants and conquer Albion. Plath describes the Atlantic and its colors, "bean green over blue."

It was after Brutus that the word *brut* first came to mean "a chronicle of British history." In her personal library, Plath owned *Wynner and Wastoure*, the Middle English poem about the founding of Britain by King Brutus. Brutus became the first king and renamed his prize "Britain" after himself, later founding the ancient city of London. Believing to have been led by the goddess Diana, who directed him to Britain in a vision, Brutus claimed Britain was the "Appointed Place for My People Israel."

So Brutus was Jewish! Who knew? *Wynner and Wastoure* sheds a little more light on the Jew references in "Daddy." Brutus was, in fact, searching for a place where King David's descendants would be free from invasion.

Originally from Italy, Brutus, whose father was Silvius, was told by a magician that his son Brutus would be the bravest and most beloved child in all of Italy. In a sort of reverse Snow White-Wicked Queen situation, the father became enraged with jealousy and had the magician killed. Brutus's mother died in childbirth, and Brutus probably lived a fearful childhood under such a tyrant, sounding like Plath's "Barely daring to breathe or Achoo." At fifteen years old, Brutus accidentally killed his father with an arrow, echoing the beginning of the second stanza:

> "Daddy, I have had to kill you. / You died before I had time."

Brutus was banished from his homeland and fled to Greece. Depending upon the source, Brutus's genealogy has been traced back to Noah, to a Roman king, and even the Greek gods. The Trojans fought and won many battles in Britain, seen in the "wars, wars, wars" of "Daddy."

Brutus's London Stone

Our friend King Brutus first set foot in the town of Totnes, in Devon, England, which is the region Plath and Hughes lived in during their time at Court Green. There, set in concrete on Fore Street, is a rock known as the Brutus Stone. People have made wishes upon the Brutus Stone for centuries, where this legendary King of Britain was said to have first stepped (Plath's "Put your foot, your root"). The granite stone looks like "one grey toe, / Big as a Frisco seal." Look up a picture of it online. Plath's description is perfect.

And then there is one of London's most ancient relics: the mysterious London Stone, which also has Brutus behind its lore. It's said to have been a Druid altarpiece for the goddess Diana; a Roman milestone; the place King Arthur's Excalibur sword was embedded; and is considered to be the "heart of London." Charles Dickens called the London Stone "That curious relic of old London," and William Shakespeare wrote about the stone in *Henry VI* when Jack Cade struck his sword upon it before leading his men in a failed rebellion.

Some believed that if the London Stone were destroyed, London would fall. Legend says the stone originated from the site where Brutus built his palace at Guildhall, which is guarded by the "Ghastly statue[s]" of the giants Gog and Magog.

Known as "Queen Elizabeth's Merlin," Dr. John Dee (1527-1608) was an alchemist and sorcerer who believed the London Stone to be so powerful that he took a sample from it for experiments. The magical London Stone was secretly housed in a wall of St. Swithin's Church until the church was bombed by the Nazis in World War II, referenced in "Daddy" with mention of Nazis, the Panzer-man, Luftwaffe, and wars. And just wait until you learn the news of the day about this stone when Plath wrote "Daddy"!

The Stone's Connections to Jews and Blake

Over the years, critics and scholars have given Sylvia Plath, a white middle-class American woman, a hard time for comparing her suffering to that of the Jews. Maybe you did too before you started to learn just how deep her poems go. Reading only the surface of Plath's poems and taking it all as mere autobiography is the biggest mistake most Plath readers make. Little by little, you are understanding the connections, though. Aren't you?

In addition to the Qabalah having roots in ancient Jewish mysticism, one must look at the great poet and artist William Blake (1757-1827) and where he shows up in Plath's "Daddy." Blake, whom Plath and Hughes both revered, imagined the groans of the execution victims at that London Stone when he wrote "To the Jews," a selection from his larger piece, *Jerusalem*. In "To the Jews," Blake examines Britain's evil and paternalistic warring roots. Blake wrote:

> "Jerusalem, the Emanation of the Giant Albion! Can it be? Is it a truth that the learned have explored? Was Britain the primitive seat of the Patriarchal Religion? […] 'All things begin and end in Albion's ancient Druid rocky shore.'"

and a little farther down, on the same plate, Blake wrote:

> Where Albion slept beneath the Fatal Tree,
> And the Druids' golden Knife
> Rioted in human gore, In Offerings of Human Life…
> They groan'd aloud on London Stone"
> —*Jerusalem*, f. 27

Incredibly, Blake's "To the Jews" even goes on to name Primrose Hill, the neighborhood in London where Plath and Hughes first lived together after she finished at Cambridge, and where Plath later returned and died.

There is yet *another* London Stone in Staines, Middlesex, which was erected in 1285 to mark the western boundary of London. This London Stone fits Plath's words:

> "Says there are a dozen or two. / So I never could tell where you / Put your foot, your root."

The London Stone became a landmark in the twelfth century, found on maps and marking the traditional place to pass laws, make proclamations, and swear oaths, but has since been moved several times ("Chuffing me off like a Jew"). And as you're starting to get the gist of how Plath's mind worked, you won't be surprised to learn that St. Swithin's Church, home of the most famous London Stone, was demolished in 1962. Surprise! In the *same month* that Plath wrote "Daddy," October 1962, the London Stone was moved to a specially constructed alcove in a wall on 111 Cannon Street, where it was placed behind an iron grate ("stuck in a barb wire snare"). This was a major news story for Londoners, and no doubt the inspiration for pulling it into "Daddy."

Whether the Brutus Stone or the London Stone, it makes sense that in "Daddy," Plath matched these tales with the queens of the tarot, with the rulers of England, and her government in London. And lest we forget, The Tower of London, of course, was known for its tortures. A favorite method was the rack, invented by the fifteenth-century Constable, the Duke of Exeter, and known as "Exeter's Daughter." Less well-known was "The Scavenger's Daughter," a method of torture that was the opposite of the rack and compressed the body. These terrible daughters, as well as all forms of horrible screws employed in the Tower, fit with the line "And a love of the rack and the screw."

The Brutal Tax Collector

What's that old saying? *The only things that are certain are death and taxes.* Everyone hates the tax collector. Tax collectors have been reviled since Biblical times, and the Bible is perhaps one of the oldest records of the Jews complaining about collectors' greed and collaboration with the Roman government. In the Bible's New Testament, Mark 12:17, Jesus is credited with saying, "Render therefore unto Caesar the things which are Caesar's; and unto God the things that are God's."

Fast-forward to 1086 C.E. Devon's town of Totnes, home of the Brutus Stone, was one of the original cities of "The Domesday Book," the great survey of England completed at the turn of that first millennium to establish the worth of all land and livestock for taxation purposes.

Paying taxes fits Plath's vampire and stake images, not for blood, not for passion, but for money. Plath had her own struggles and complaints about paying taxes, and perhaps only scholars in the archives know that she was perhaps a little less than legal about it. Her tax avoidance strategies included forwarding checks to her mother to deposit into an account in the U.S., which can be seen in her letters to Aurelia Plath around this time. In "Daddy," Plath vents the villagers' feelings about the governmental daddy, the tax man. It won't be a surprise to you, then, to learn that Ted Hughes was a direct descendant of Guillaume de Ferriere, the Master of Horse for William the Conqueror and the implementer of The Domesday Book!

In "Daddy," Plath has cheekily drawn a line from Britain's first tax collector directly to her evil husband, bringing the two together as one. She could leave Hughes, but his tradition was ages old and would remain a threat.

The judgment of the tax assessors was final and known as "Domesday," the Day of Judgement (British spelling) and the origin of the colloquial term *Doomsday*. Plath wrote a poem called "Doomsday," found in her Juvenilia in *The Collected Poems of Sylvia Plath*.

The English town of Totnes boasts a Norman castle, fitting the many German references in this poem, built to keep the rebellious local people under control by their medieval feudal lords. Totnes is also home to the ancient Leech Well (again fitting the blood-drinking symbolism of "Daddy") where lepers went to cleanse themselves of their disease. I don't have to tell you by now that Plath was a master of circular meanings and of milking every possible signification and reference out of her words and symbolism.

Other British Kings

While the focus of "Daddy" is on queens, these ladies do usually seem to be attached to kings, don't they? The ten-centuries-old British royal family must not be ignored in the poem "Daddy," because the British Empire and both world wars were led by British kings. King George V was staunchly anti-German after Britain went to war in 1914; so much so that they changed their own German last name from the German Saxe-Coburg and Gotha to the English Windsor. During World War I, all German-sounding titles, buildings and family names of British subjects were changed to anglicized versions, to appease nationalist feelings ("I could hardly speak. / I thought every German was you. / And the language obscene"). When King George V died, his son Edward VIII took the crown, but then soon abdicated, leaving it to his brother Prince Albert so Edward could marry the twice-divorced Wallis Simpson. Prince Albert took the title of King George VI. A Freemason like Plath's father Otto, King Edward VII was a Grand Master, and his grandsons Edward VIII and George VI were Masons, and so was Winston Churchill.

Before becoming king, Albert was called "the Industrial Prince," touring coal mines, factories and rail yards, fitting Plath's engine reference. Albert had a bad stammer, echoed in the fifth and sixth stanzas of "Daddy." He was the subject of the Academy Award-winning film, *The King's Speech* (2010).

King George VI worked to dissolve the British Empire and was appalled when told he could not shake hands with blacks in South Africa. He referred to his South African bodyguards as "The Gestapo." Because of the King's poor health, Princess Elizabeth and her husband traveled all over the world, taking the place of the king and queen and reflecting the world travel of "Daddy."

In 1947, Britain's Princess Elizabeth married Prince Philip of Greece and Denmark. Philip's sisters had married German noblemen with Nazi links, and, very soon after World War II, this did not sit well with much of the United Kingdom. Harold Macmillan wrote that the Queen has indeed "the heart and stomach of a man," traits of the Queen of Swords tarot card. Queen Elizabeth II inherited rulership over 16 sovereign states in 1952, including segregated South Africa, when her own Daddy died.

In Plath's copy of *The Portable James Joyce*, she underlined an editor's introductory comments:

> "Where the father is the embodiment of nationality in Stephen's recollections, his mother embodies religion."

Plath took that idea of the father embodying nationality to heart in "Daddy."

Nazis at Nauset

So, you've got the Brutus connection, and you see the London Stone, and you've absorbed all that stuff about the queens and myth and Qabalah. How do the Nazis fit in? They're surely in the poem, right? With all the mention of German and wars and a Panzer-man? Of course they are. But probably not in the way you expected it.

The only attack on U.S. soil to occur in World War I was in July 1918 at Nauset Beach, in the town of Orleans, Massachusetts, on Cape Cod and not far from where Plath grew up. There "In the waters off beautiful Nauset," an Imperial German U-boat, which is the Anglicized version of the German word *U-Boot*, meaning submarine, opened fire on the town and several merchant vessels nearby. The U-boat's periscope would look like Plath's "head in the freakish Atlantic," and Nauset is named in Plath's poem. The Germanic origins and the black boot imagery of Plath's "Daddy" contribute to understanding this connection, as well as to realizing the confusion Plath must have felt about her family's heritage, both loving and hating her Germanic roots. The only other time this area of Nauset faced attack was by the British in the War of 1812. British Navy uniforms were navy blue, and German Nazi uniforms were "bean green," explaining Plath's colors of the pouring waters. The British enemy element adds further metaphorical comparison for Plath with her British husband. But you already picked up on that, didn't you?

Apartheid in "Daddy"

The suffering and mistreatment of blacks in South Africa present another new meaning to the blackness of "Daddy": In 1962, the South African government stripped blacks entirely of their rights and gave the people's land to those "poor and white." This Nazi-like racism prevailed ("Not God but a swastika / So black no sky could squeak through"). The "boot in the face" was typical of the treatment of black South Africans and "the villagers" were the original black South Africans.

Why would Plath have an interest in South Africa? Plath's favorite Cambridge professor, Dorothea Krook, grew up and was educated in South Africa, and she and Krook's Cape Town friend, Wendy Christie, were some of Plath's best female friends at Cambridge. Additionally, Plath made many new South African friends in her first semester at Cambridge. When she returned to America for her year of teaching, Plath wrote of wanting to contribute to help African students who suffered through apartheid through Smith College's Relief Committee in 1958, and she wrote in April 1960 that the Sharpeville Massacres of black protestors in South Africa were causing upset in Britain.

Beginning in 1948, South African apartheid had been going on for seven years when Plath became conscious of it, fitting the length of time in the poem's second-to-last stanza. How Plath might have marveled at the coincidence of South African poet Dennis Brutus's (1924-2009) name, and his famous collection of prize-winning poetry, *Sirens, Knuckles, Boots* (1963), published in the year Plath died, about his fellow blacks under apartheid! Perhaps she had seen an early copy of it. It is not impossible, because Dennis Brutus wrote a poem remembering Ted Hughes, called "A Poem for Ted Hughes," published in South Africa's *The Daily News*, 25 March 2009. The two poets were often anthologized together.

The coincidences, if you still believe in such things, just keep on coming.

Africa: The Dark Continent

In Victorian times, Africa was referred to as "The Dark Continent," with all the negative connotations the British associated with darkness. Letters tell us that in Cambridge, Plath and her friends discussed the Belgian Congo over tea in mid-November. She had friends of color, as well as professors and friends from South Africa. The continent of Africa plays front and center throughout several of Plath's intended mirrors for "Daddy," the first being the Balobedu tribe of South Africa, who have their own kingdom with a female ruler, the Rain Queen.

The Rain Queen

In *Winter Pollen*, Ted Hughes wrote of Plath's love of Paul Radin's *African Folktales*, and there is a high probability that she knew about and enjoyed the African Balobedu's Rain Queen myth, included in the book. In Radin's telling of the Ekoi story, "How The First Rain Came," a royal daughter is saved from a terrible husband by her king father. The Balobedu tribe's Rain Queen was first made popular by the Victorian author H. Rider Haggard, in his best-selling books, *King Solomon's Mines* (1885), which introduced his famous fictional adventurer and white hunter, Allan Quartermain, and *She: A History of Adventure (*1887). The latter novel has never been out of print.

The Rain Queen is known as an extremely powerful magician, able to make rain and cause drought upon her enemies. Some legends say that the lineage began when a young woman, Dzugundini, was impregnated by her father, the last Mugudo, or male leader. This idea of incest is another echo of the Electra complex, and suggests the black of African skin and Plath's disconnection from the "root." If you really want to push the symbolism, *root* might also take its slang meaning for *penis*. Dzugundini gave birth to the first Rain Queen, and there have been six Rain Queens since 1800.

The Rain Queen is not allowed to marry, but instead has many "wives." Her male sexual partners are chosen by a royal council and were usually close relatives, to maintain pure blood, the same idea of endogamy that the Nazis embraced.

In times of South African drought, rituals for rain included the sacrifice of a black bull which symbolized rain clouds, the use of powerful medicines containing human remains, and the beating of royal graves to berate ancestors for not taking care of them. In "Daddy," Plath gives us the blackness, the bones and "the sack." In the 1600s, the Balobedu people separated from their Karanga Empire to be led by their Rain Queen.

The Rain Queen was to abstain from all social functions, remain in isolation, and she communicated through envoys, never able to speak with anyone directly and echoing the fifth stanza of "Daddy" again. She was expected to commit suicide when her eldest daughter came of age to rule, which sounds like what most people interpret in "Daddy" as Plath's suicide attempt in the twelfth stanza.

The third Rain Queen, who ruled in Plath's time, refused her directive to drink poison, commit suicide, and give up the throne. She intended to rule "even at the age of 80," but her daughter took over in 1959, ruling until 1980. There have been two Rain Queens since, but the last Queen's daughter was fathered by a commoner, and the tradition seems to have come to an end. Evidence of the Rain Queen's great powers is her lush garden, filled with the world's largest cycad plants. A perfect metaphor for the queen herself, these plants also interbreed. Perhaps most interesting about the Rain Queen Dynasty is that the queen's succession is matrilineal, and men are not able to inherit the throne.

Polish Connections

What about the Polish stuff? How does that fit in?

After the Battle of Vienna in 1683, King of Poland John III Sobieski paraphrased Shakespeare's famous quotation from *Julius Caesar*, saying, "Venimus, Vidimus, Deus Vincit," meaning, "We came, we saw, God conquered." This king also appears in the astronomy mirror of this poem. Sobieski won a great battle against the Ottoman Empire which had conquered much of Europe, Asia, and the Mediterranean. Yes, this fits the references to Vienna, "Polack," German, Polish towns and all the wars of the poem "Daddy."

The capture of Vienna had been one of the Ottoman Empire's goals. Previously, there had been peace from the Peace of Vasvár treaty for twenty years (twenty being another time marker in the twelfth stanza of this poem), but the Ottomans decided to reclaim their land ("And get back, back, back to you"). The Battle of Vienna marked the end of the over-proud Ottoman Empire's expansion into Europe. The Ottoman Empire entered World War I in an alliance with Germany that was to be the downfall of both empires. As Plath's father's first name was "Otto," she may have enjoyed that she had yet another "Daddy" association. By now, you see that this poem has more layers than a piece of German *Schichttorte*.[2]

Sigmund Freud, Father of Psychoanalysis

You knew this was coming: Not to be forgotten is the "Daddy" of psychoanalysis himself, Sigmund Freud, who proclaimed that the "Electra complex" is a female's psychosexual neurosis which arises from a sexual attachment to her father. "Daddy" is full of Freud, who was born a Jew in the Austrian Empire ("The snows of the Tyrol") part of what is now the Czech Republic, bordering Poland ("in the Polish town"). He spent a great deal of his life in Vienna ("the clear

---

[2] A cake with twenty layers.

beer of Vienna") and spoke German ("In the German tongue"). Because of his German heritage, Freud was "Not God" as doctors under the red cross of medicine are sometimes hailed, "but a swastika."[3]

You might recall that Plath introduced a recording for the BBC of "Daddy," downplaying its power by saying it was about "a girl with an Electra complex. Her father died while she thought he was God." This Electra complex idea certainly echoes and reinforces the Rain Queen's presence in "Daddy," as well as all the myth associated with the queens, both mentioned earlier. While scholars had no problem accepting "Daddy" as an expression of Freud's Electra complex, it seems no one bothered to look beyond this image, to see this poem as partly a reflection of Freud's character. Now, the words "you can lie back now" become the analyst talking to his patient on the couch.

Plath's line, "I could hardly speak," is a reference, among other things, to Freud's famous "talking cure." Aurelia Plath, Sylvia's mother, mentioned in an interview that when Sylvia had her emotional breakdown in college, she went through a phase during which she could hardly read or write. When she was able to read again, she turned to the writings of Freud, seeking the answers to her psychological complexes.

But back to Herr Freud: In 1933, the Nazis took control of Germany and publicly burned Freud's books, among other writers' works, as a statement against Jews. Freud's four sisters were later killed by the Nazis in concentration camps.

In Hampstead, North London, in front of the Tavistock Clinic, near where Sigmund Freud lived with his daughter, Anna (another interesting echo of the Electra complex), there is a "Ghastly statue" of the doctor. The sculptor carved only Freud's right boot, appearing as

---

[3] In Kundalini Yoga, which Ted Hughes practiced, the "Swastika Center" dwells at the very top of the chakra system of the subconscious mind. Poet and friend of Hughes, Robert Graves, notes the swastika represents "The fullest extent of sovereignty." The right-handed wheel was considered lucky. The left-handed one, which was adopted by the Nazis, unlucky.

"one grey toe/ Big as a Frisco seal." Many pictures of this statue can be found online.

Of all Freud's concepts, his idea of *working-through* most completely sums up the role of the patient in analysis. Working-through is not about analytic technique, but rather, the labor of the patient. The patient works through two phases: recognizing resistances, which is insight; and overcoming resistances, which is change. In his 1914 paper, "Remembering, Repeating and Working-Through (Further Recommendations on the Technique of Psycho-Analysis II)", Freud defines the id-resistance seen in Plath's first line; the compulsion to repeat, again seen in *you do not do,* as well as the repetition of the words *wars, Ich, Jew, Taroc pack, Panzer-man, brute, back, I do,* and of course, the name *Daddy*. Additionally, there is the death instinct, with many instances of this throughout the poem from the second stanza on. Ultimately, Freud's "working-through" technique is a will for recovery ("I used to pray to recover you") through a will to remember.

Plath surely realized that Freud was a metaphor for his work, and vice-versa. Getting back to where we started, Freud was also a Freemason, again like Plath's father, Otto. Freud's paper, *Totem and Taboo*, hypothesized the murder of the tyrannical father of the primal horde by his children. The paper's premise is that a sense of guilt is the emotional foundation of an emerging civilization. The point is that the West was built upon the backs of slaves and people of color.

You can see it all in "Daddy" by now (and yet, there is more!). This layering of interrelated themes is the nuts and bolts of spellcasting. It is the way Plath quietly but powerfully gets in our heads and stays there.

With Freud in mind, "Daddy" is ultimately about releasing the frightening primitive subconscious *Id* that is kept in check, and even killed, by the *Superego*. The Superego arises as a resolution to the Oedipus/Electra complex. Freud believed that it represents an internal father and his prohibitions, and therefore manifests itself as conscience and a sense of guilt.

The first lines of "Daddy" are the strict imperatives of Freud's restrictive Superego. The Superego seeks to maintain purity, risks nothing to keep and enforce order, and it does not give in to the primal. Therefore, it hardly lives, being "poor and white, / Barely daring to breathe or Achoo." Plath once read this poem aloud to her friend Clarissa Roche, and the two of them were said to have exploded into peals of laughter at its nursery-rhyme quality. Roche explained in a film documentary that "the 'Daddy' is the daddy inside of her, *not* her beloved father."

"I was ten when they buried you," is near the age of eight when Plath lost her father, but also, more likely, it was the age when she lost her ability to feel playful, free and uncontrolled, allowing her Freudian Id to break free. "I'll never speak to God again," Plath had said after her father died in November of 1940.

God, for Plath, was the spirit of the subconscious. "At twenty I tried to die / And get back, back, back to you" was her effort, the mystic's effort, to kill the ego—physically or psychologically. But Plath was always rescued and mended with doctors and shock therapy ("And they stuck me together with glue").

The unconscious Id is powerful, nonsensical, uncontrolled and frightening, and we have the fear and "gobbledygoo" in this poem. Plath wrote of reading Freud's *Mourning and Melancholia*, calling it "An almost exact description of my feelings and reasons for suicide: a transferred murderous impulse from my mother onto myself: the 'vampire' metaphor Freud uses, 'draining the ego'."

Sigmund Freud's student and a famous psychologist in his own right, Carl Jung, also used the vampire symbolism we see in Plath's "Daddy" to describe life-sucking personalities. It is here that Plath explains her vampire metaphor in "Daddy." Consider that Plath's "Seven years, if you want to know" might also come to mean how long it took her to understand and absorb this knowledge. While Plath had made references about sounding "Freudian" in her journals, it wasn't until 1957 that she wrote of actually reading Freud seriously. In 1962, when "Daddy" was written, she would have been absorbing his school of thought for nearly seven years. The "Daddy" Plath had to kill was Freud's male-chauvinistic focus on psychology, as well as the primal, childish Id which Freud identified within us all.

So you were right when you thought "Daddy" was a somewhat feminist poem. You just didn't know that it was also a freedom-for-oppressed-people and a freedom-from-repressed-emotions poem. Now you know.

CHAPTER EIGHT

Fifth Mirror: Astrology and Astronomy

The Fixed Stars that Govern a Life

While astrology and astronomy are two very different things, in ancient times they were one and the same. Plath's journal entries, poems, and letters have echoed her appreciation for the stars and stargazing since she was in the sixth grade. Ted Hughes was a serious practitioner of astrology; he calculated every auspicious date for mailing out poems to be published, and credited the stars for every event in his life, including his meeting and marrying Plath.

Throughout their marriage, Plath wrote often of her admiration of Hughes's ability to write horoscopes and natal charts. Hughes's friend Lucas Myers believed Hughes saw astrology "not as a science, but as an instrument for intuitive insights," and claimed that Hughes wrote him from the U.S. during his time with Plath, stating that vision, or controlled dreaming while awake, was common in the Middle Ages. It was Hughes's goal to awaken this sleeping gift.

Sobieski's Shield and Other Stars

Hang on; we are not finished with the stars yet: One of the newer constellations to have been identified was *Scutum Sobiescianum*, found in 1684 by Polish astronomer Johannes Hevelius. The name is Latin for *Sobieski's shield* and given in honor of the Polish King Sobieski (remember him from the History mirror?) seven years after the king's victory (and there is *seven* again). Scutum is comprised nearly a dozen stars (Plath's "dozen or two") found in the Milky Way, between the tail of the Serpent and the head of Sagittarius. Some characteristics of Scutum even sound like the History mirror of "Daddy," but we have to rein this in somewhere, so that's for you to look up if you are interested.

The Queens' Zodiac

In the tarot, each one of the four queens is assigned to the zodiac sign corresponding to her element. The active Queen of Wands associates with fire, and the fire signs are Aries, Leo, and Sagittarius. The emotional Queen of Cups represents the water signs of Pisces, Cancer, and Scorpio. The worldly Queen of Pentacles represents the earth signs of Taurus, Virgo, and Capricorn. And the sharp Queen of Swords represents the air signs of Aquarius, Gemini, and Libra.

Plath's "dozen" in "Daddy" of course means the number twelve. Twelve is an important mystical number: The zodiac hinges upon it, with the months of the year, and twelve zodiac signs. Twelve is also the number of disciples and apostles in all major religions.

Black Saturn

Enough with the stars. Let's talk planets.

Associated with the tarot queens' rank's third station on the Qabalah Tree of Life is the planet Saturn. Saturn and its corresponding humour[4] in alchemy, black bile, are linked with the emotion of melancholy. Saturn's color is black, connecting back to the alchemical mirror of this poem, and the planet is associated with the element lead, an essential mineral for war materials and ammunition. Lead makes an excellent shield against radiation, touching back to the shield constellation of Scutum.

Astrologers believe Saturn represents the undesirable elements in human society, much as the Nazis viewed the Jewish people. Saturn is regarded as a tyrannical father by Gnostics, and they believe the planet to govern over those obsessed with rigid enforcement of the law. This same idea of a dominating, difficult father is said to represent Saturn-influenced individuals' astrological charts. The planet is considered to be cold and dry, casting these traits as well. In Vedic astrology, Saturn and Jupiter, while usually neutral, become enemies when in close relationship to one another. Associated with the middle or third finger, black Saturn is said to bring rain—another connection back to the Rain Queen. Whew! What a killjoy.

---

[4] Greek physician Hippocrates (ca. 460 BCE – 370 BCE) is credited with developing the theory of four humours that influence the body and its emotions: blood, yellow bile, black bile, and phlegm.

CHAPTER NINE

Sixth Mirror: The Arts and Humanities

Hail, Caesar!

> The fault, dear Brutus, is not in our stars, but in ourselves, that we are underlings.
> —William Shakespeare, *Julius Caesar*

The joining of Britain's King Brutus with the Queens rank in the tarot is made through William Shakespeare's great literary work, *Julius Caesar*. Characters include:
- Julius Caesar, who bears all the characteristics of "Daddy" in Plath's poem
- Brutus, discussed in History and the World Events mirror. "The brute/Brute heart"
- Cleopatra, famous African queen; royalty

- Mark Antony, who with Brutus, killed his dear friend Caesar for the sake of Rome and then committed suicide ("If I've killed one man, I've killed two")
- Cinna, the poet who exposes mob psychology comparable to Nazism

In Shakespeare's *Julius Caesar*, Cinna the poet is attacked, revealing the subconscious desire people have to go along with the masses. It is easily comparable to what the Jews or the gypsies suffered from the Nazi movement of the twentieth century. We saw a brief appearance of Caesar also in the History and World Events mirror of "Daddy," about paying tax collectors. But that's only the beginning of literary correspondences to Plath's poem "Daddy":

Daddy's *Heart of Darkness*

Wait a minute! I get what you've shown me so far, but how many novels can Plath pack into one poem?

I found four. Maybe there are others. When you read on, you will see that each one of these novels I name perfectly fits into Plath's "Daddy," and each novel meant a lot to her.

Even more relevant to "Daddy" than *Julius Caesar*, however, is the 1902 novella *Heart of Darkness*, a story Ted Hughes recounts reading aloud to Plath in his book, *Birthday Letters*. Written by Polish writer Joseph Conrad (the Polish themes again), Conrad's *Heart of Darkness* is set in 1900-1920, coinciding with World War I, and King George V and VI's reigns. Plath might have gotten a spark of the idea from the October 1962 issue of *Encounter* magazine, a literary journal she read and that her work appeared in earlier that year. During the month she wrote "Daddy," *Encounter* featured author Michael Hamburger's story about Conrad, "A Craving for Hell."

Much has been written about author Joseph Conrad and his parallels to his character Charles Marlow in *Heart of Darkness*. Conrad did not speak a word of English until he was in his twenties, sounding like the fifth and sixth stanzas of "Daddy." Among other adventures of his young life that fed his literary work, Conrad became the captain of a Congo steamboat, fitting the engine and the wandering that has also been compared with Jews. There is also the famous "Grove of Death" scene, in which Marlow comes upon a boiler and railway car off the tracks, described as "decaying machinery" which serves as a dark metaphor for the starving Africans working as slaves for the British. Conrad witnessed horrible atrocities against the African people that were all portrayed in *Heart of Darkness*, which labeled the author both a racist ("your Aryan eye") and a humanitarian exposing the shocking truth.

In *Heart of Darkness*, Charles Marlow begins his journey in London on the Thames River, and down through Plath's "Atlantic." Marlow considers London "one of the dark places on earth" and muses over how the ancient Romans who took over and built up Britain were probably not so different from the Belgians and British in the Belgian Congo. He says of the Romans, "They were conquerors, and for that you want only brute force—" recalling Plath's "the brute/Brute heart of a brute like you," as well as the history of King Brutus. The "stake in your fat black heart" now, therefore, translates to the territory of Africa.

Marlow is fascinated by a character called Kurtz, who is chief of the Inner Station and a German-named ivory trader ("In the German tongue"). Kurtz has a reputation as a genius, talented in many arts, and he possesses a cruel streak. These are traits that run all throughout the poem "Daddy." Throughout the story, Marlow continually hears Kurtz's voice and others ("The voices just can't worm through"):

> "A voice. He was very little more than a voice. And I heard—him—it—this voice—other voices—all of them were so little more than voice—and the memory of that time itself lingers around me, impalpable, like a dying vibration of one immense jabber, silly, atrocious, sordid, savage, or simply mean, without any kind of sense. Voices, voices—".

There is a sense of Plath's "gobbledygook" in this quotation, too. Kurtz's fiancée, back home in Britain, is naïve about the crimes of her country against the African people, and about her lover's darker side ("Every woman adores a Fascist"). She is so much so, that at the end of the story she believes Kurtz's last words were her name when in fact they were "The horror! The horror!"

The Freudian *Finnegans Wake*

You've seen some mentions of James Joyce previously, and how Plath emulated Joyce's writing methods. Plath quoted Joyce from *Finnegans Wake* in her journals:

> "and It's old and old it's sad and old it's sad and weary I go back to you, my cold father, my cold mad father, my cold mad feary father."

It's almost impossible not to hear her line from "Daddy," "And get back, back, back to you" sculpted from those words.

Many believe that *Finnegans Wake* was an attempt to recreate the experience of sleep and dreams—very much in line with Freud's work. In 1946, Laszlo Moholy-Nagy diagrammed the book, showing its mystical themes in line with the works of Dante's cosmology, Homer's *The Odyssey*, Joyce's own *Ulysses*, Shakespeare, and the Egyptian *Book of the Dead*. Interestingly, Book II of *Finnegans Wake* features the character, HCE, who proclaims his incestuous desire for young girls. There are also Nazi and Gestapo themes in *Finnegans Wake*.

Plath's first undergraduate thesis was originally going to be about the work of James Joyce, and Plath's protagonist in her novel *The Bell Jar*, Esther Greenwood, wanted to write her thesis on *Finnegans Wake*. Joyce modernized Homer's *Odyssey* in his fictional masterpiece, *Ulysses*, in 1922, and this was another favorite novel of Plath and Hughes. Also an occultist himself, Joyce belonged to the Dublin Hermetic Society, founded by W.B. Yeats. Plath and Hughes both adored Joyce, and were in fact intentionally married on June 16, 1956—*Ulysses*' romantic "Bloomsday."

The Silver Pencil

And finally, the icing on the fictional cake:

Ever since she was a little girl, reading must have seemed magical to young Sylvia Plath. From *Little Women* to *Middlemarch*, Plath read the story of her own life, sometimes down to the smallest details, recorded in someone else's fictional tale. In her books, now kept in archives, many these amazing coincidences and her excited observations are revealed in Plath's underlinings, stars, and annotations.

In late December 1944, Plath waded through Alice Dalgliesh's thinly-veiled partial autobiography, *The Silver Pencil*, probably as part of a reading club because Plath included notes and treasured maxims from this book in a special notebook. The historical children's novel thrilled her enough that she read it again eight months later.

In *The Silver Pencil*, Janet, a British colonist growing up in Trinidad, falls in love with literature, reading *Little Women* and *Ladies' Home Journal*, and writing her own stories and poems. Just like Plath. Her hard-to-please father dies young when Janet is the same age at which Plath lost her father. But before the fictional father died, he had given Janet the gift of a silver pencil, which he had placed atop a German Christmas tree. *German!* I mean, come on! How much more Plathian can you get? The story is set in 1939, as Britain declares war on Germany. From the children's novel:

> "Every Sunday Mr. Wilson tells us God is love and God is kind," she said, her voice trembling. "But He isn't, because He has taken away my father. Other girls don't lose their fathers. Why do I have to?"

The book continues with Janet speaking like a childhood version of Sylvia Plath:

"[…] rebelliously. Then, flatly, 'I don't love God.'"

There is a final moment in Chapter 22 of this story that contains the closing spirit of "Daddy":

> "Men!" Janet said fiercely, "I'm going to get myself a nice job in a girls' boarding school. Then I won't see a man from one year's end to another. I'm *through*."

The Silver Pencil is an amusing final nod to the metal lead, or the misconception that there is lead within pencils, as well as displaying a young girl's first feminist feelings. The final words of the character Janet and Plath's poem are the same: through. In the English language, through is a preposition, an adverb, and an adjective. In "Daddy," it is used informally as a verb. Plath used through this way in one other angry and feministic *Ariel* poem, "Lesbos":

> "In New York, Hollywood, the men said: 'Through? / Gee baby, you are rare.'"

Also in "Lesbos," Plath writes:

> "The bastard's a girl."

In "Daddy," it's:

> "Daddy, daddy, you bastard,"

—but this narrator is just as fatherless no matter which character we assign to her.

The Silver Pencil also likely introduced Plath to many historical themes and details she would absorb and carry with her in later years. Maybe Sylvia Plath even saw a little bit of her name in the title. Did you catch the *Silv* and the *P*?

The Silver Pencil, for Plath as a girl, might have helped explain the boldness of American women, from their pioneer heritages and wilderness, as contrasted with the sheltered girls of Victorian England. Plath might have, in some way, understood British colonialism because her own city of Boston had been part of a British colony for 150 years. This children's novel takes a close look at themes and images that would infuse Plath's later poetry, including "Daddy." We see colonialism, the death of King Edward VII and the reign of King George V, and an almost infinite number of eerie correspondences, which are covered in my forthcoming biography of Plath and Hughes' mysticism, *The Magician's Girl*.

What makes the poem "Daddy" one of Sylvia Plath's finest works is that when the good guy and bad guy are switched, whether it's Otto or Ted, God or herself, black man or white, the queens are skillfully woven through each magical facet. They create the perfect alchemy and ultimately rule the show.

CHAPTER NINE

Decoding Sylvia Plath's "Daddy" in the Classroom

Teaching Guide

Thank you for considering *Decoding Sylvia Plath's "Daddy"* for your classroom. This section is a guide for expanding upon Plath's poem "Daddy" for an interactive, stimulating and fun experience. This class plan may be adapted for traditional classrooms, online courses, and creative writing workshops, and it has been tested in actual classrooms for two years with great success.[5] Please feel free to modify this plan to suit your own unique needs, and please, please share your ideas and suggestions with the author at DecodingSylviaPlath@gmail.com.

For the last fifty years, Sylvia Plath has unfortunately been known more for her history of mental instability and tragic suicide than for her brilliance. There are two primary reasons for this: First, her single published novel, *The Bell Jar*, is continually and unfortunately read only as autobiography. Secondly, Plath's poetry, especially the *Ariel* collection, opened up the new genre of confessional poetry and was, therefore, read also as autobiography. This is regardless of her husband Ted Hughes's claims that this was not confessional poetry, but rather a mystical work "of the highest tradition."

What my first book, *Fixed Stars Govern a Life: Decoding Sylvia Plath* set out to prove is that Plath was a great deal more than a depressive and unstable, angry suicide, and that her work is a great deal more than autobiography. Through *FSGL*, and this *Decoding Sylvia Plath* series, you will learn that each of Plath's poems is a synthesis of multiple perspectives contributing to a greater mystical structure and that Sylvia Plath was possibly the greatest genius in literature from the last hundred years.

Should you decide to work through the poems covered in *Fixed Stars Govern a Life: Decoding Sylvia Plath*, Volume One, you will soon understand how one and all poems relate to the whole of the Qabalah Tree of Life. Check Amazon and other distributors for

---

[5] Online courses using the *Fixed Stars Govern a Life: Decoding Sylvia Plath, Volume One* text (2014, Stephen F. Austin State University Press) at Lindenwood University's graduate Creative Writing Program, 2015-2017.

Decoding books and class plans for the first twenty-two poems in *Ariel,* for which *Decoding* books are forthcoming. Some copies of *FSGL* are still available online as well, although now it is out of print.

If you are exploring "Daddy" with your class without first reading *Fixed Stars Govern a Life*, you might want to peruse the introductory readings "What Set Me Going," "Author's Notes on How to Read these Interpretations," and "Understanding the Mirrors," that begin this program. These can be found online at no cost here: https://lindenwood.academia.edu/JuliaGordonBramer. It might be helpful to understand my process as to how I decoded "Daddy," because these findings are new and original at the time of this writing.

As an instructor, you might want to structure the first class around these introductory readings. This will help to familiarize students with the language, provide introductory images of the tarot and Qabalah Tree of Life (also found in the beginning section of *FSGL*), as well as some biographical material on Sylvia Plath (suggested supplemental materials follow, as does an appendix with a sample syllabus, student projects, and more). Smaller classes might be able to get through more information more quickly than large groups.

If the instructor is interested in focusing on the order of the *Ariel* poems, or on a poem's imagery and meaning within the corresponding tarot card, you can choose to bring in actual tarot cards, or simply project tarot card images on a screen. The tarot cards presented should be either the Rider-Waite or Universal Waite Tarot Decks (the latter are colored more brightly), both featuring artwork by Pamela Colman Smith. The Rider-Waite Tarot was the deck that Ted Hughes most likely purchased for Plath's birthday in 1956, and the deck that Plath used, given its availability in England at the time and its strong correlation with the *Ariel* poems.

As instructor, the availability of *FSGL* or other *Decoding Sylvia Plath* books, your amount of class time, the number of times the class meets, and number of classes within a semester all figure into how many poems you decide to cover, as well as how many exercises and which ones you use.

This class plan is a living document, and I will continually be incorporating new ideas and sharing teaching methods that seem appropriate. In addition to sharing best practices on the *FSGL* website, www.fixedstarsgovernalife.com, please feel free to write me with your comments and ideas for improvement.

> "And now you try
> Your handful of notes;
> The clear vowels rise like balloons."
> —Sylvia Plath, "Morning Song"

Thank you,
Julia Gordon-Bramer

Suggested Supplemental Materials:

[Online classes may wish to post these links]

Rider-Waite Tarot deck images may be found here: http://en.wikipedia.org/wiki/Rider-Waite_tarot_deck. The twenty-two major arcana cards correspond with Plath's first twenty-two poems in *Ariel*, as explained in *Fixed Stars Govern a Life*, Volume One.

The Rider-Waite and Universal Waite Tarot decks may be purchased through U.S. Games. They can be found online, in many bookstores and occult shops, or on Amazon.com.

PBS *Voices and Visions* documentary on Sylvia Plath: https://www.youtube.com/watch?v=wmamNSa3sP8 (one hour)

Audio interview with Sylvia Plath: https://www.youtube.com/watch?v=g2lMsVpRh5c With Peter Orr of the British Council, 1962. (time: 14:10) The transcript may be read here: http://www.english.illinois.edu/maps/poets/m_r/plath/orrinterview.htm.

A Skype interview with author Julia Gordon-Bramer may be scheduled at no cost with your class or book club to discuss the course material, Gordon-Bramer's personal experiences in decoding Plath, and more. Schedules permitting, this might include free tarot card readings for students.

Email: DecodingSylviaPlath@gmail.com for more information.

Recommended follow-up reading:

Fixed Stars Govern a Life: Decoding Sylvia Plath, Volume One by Julia Gordon-Bramer. 2014, Stephen F. Austin State University Press, or forthcoming *Decoding* books focusing on individual poems in *Ariel*.

Her Husband, by Diane Middlebrook. 2003, Penguin Books.

Wintering: A Novel of Sylvia Plath, by Kate Moses. 2003, Anchor Books.

Birthday Letters, by Ted Hughes. 1998, Farrar, Straus and Giroux.

Required Text:

Ariel: The Restored Edition, by Sylvia Plath, 2004 HarperCollins (**Important:** any editions of *Ariel* before 2004 present the poems in a different order and are not suitable for understanding the *Fixed Stars Govern a Life* system.)

Decoding Sylvia Plath's "Daddy," by Julia Gordon-Bramer. 2017, Magi Press.

Key Goals and Benefits for Students from this Coursework:

- To demonstrate and create opportunities to teach inductive reasoning in both reading and writing.
- To understand the structure of the contemporary poem, and especially a Sylvia Plath poem.
- To understand, identify, and interpret symbolism in poetry.
- To be able to unpack a poem and discover the other various meanings and influences beneath a poem's literal and most superficial meaning.
- To expand students' reading and writing vocabulary.
- To gain an introductory knowledge of some of the more popular schools of mysticism and how they complement and inter-relate with other occult systems.
- To encourage students' creative expression.

Class Plan: The Brutal Complexes and Queens of Sylvia Plath's "Daddy"

Reading Assignment:

"Daddy," by Sylvia Plath. From *Ariel: The Restored Edition* (2004, HarperPerennial Modern Classics), pages 74-76.

Decoding Sylvia Plath's "Daddy," by Julia Gordon-Bramer. 2017, Magi Press.

Class warm-up activity:

Familiarize the group with the poem "Daddy" by Sylvia Plath, and share initial impressions.

Instructor notes:

The instructor should review background information ("What You Should Know Going In" and "About the Poem 'Daddy'" from *Decoding Sylvia Plath's "Daddy"*).

Plath wrote "Daddy" on October 12, 1962. Consider the historical context of her world events at the time (post-World War II; Cuban Missile Crisis; apartheid in South Africa, and so on). The instructor might want to review newspaper headlines from online sources.

Occult and Plath Vocabulary:

Be sure students know and can define the following words, and know something about the meaning and history behind the words that name locations. For non-location words, consider researching word origins, and archaic and obsolete definitions. For location words, students should have at least a general sense of why Plath mentions these places, where they are and what they might mean to her and others *[Note: upper and lower case is Plath's, and not necessarily standard]*:

Frisco
Nauset
Dachau
Auschwitz
Belsen
Tyrol
Vienna
Chuffing
Brute
Fascist
Luftwaffe
Panzer
swastika
Meinkampf
gypsy
Taroc
Cleft

Teaching Tip:

Line breaks, or *enjambment*, is when a line in a poem continues into the next line without a pause or break with punctuation. This effect gives a poem other meanings, especially when the reader pauses at the end of a line. Look at Plath's enjambment in "Daddy," and explore enjambment used by other poets.

In-Class Activity:

[Online courses might do this via discussion board]

Traditional Classrooms: In small groups or as a whole class, have one student read "Daddy" aloud to the group. Next, have another student read it, attempting to present it differently. Have fun with it, and encourage presenters to be as theatrical as they wish. Discuss and note differences in poetic delivery, inflection, and if any particular words or themes stood out with one person reading and not with another. Why or why not? An outstanding recording of Plath herself reading this poem can be found on YouTube.

Online: Students should read the poem aloud, and they might want to record themselves. Suggest that another friend or family member read this too, for comparison. If sound files can be uploaded to school software, students might want to hear each other read this work. Some people have recorded themselves reading Plath's work on YouTube, and this too can be a source for different presentations.

Key Themes:

As a group, identify the most obvious themes in Plath's "Daddy," then break them down into the major themes of the mirrors:

- **Tarot and Qabalah Mirror:** The queens of the tarot (in reverse); racism; Jews and gypsies; chess queens
- **Alchemical Mirror:** killing the ego; lead
- **Mythology Mirror:** Clytemnestra; Helen of Troy; Penelope/Atalanta; Omphale/Thetis/Medea; Telamon
- **History and World Events Mirror:** Brutus; London Stone; Tax Collectors; British Royalty; Nazis in U.S. waters; apartheid; Africa; Rain Queens; King Sobieski of Poland; Sigmund Freud
- **Astronomy and Astrology Mirror:** Sobieski's Shield; Saturn
- **Arts and the Humanities Mirror:** Shakespeare's *Julius Caesar*; Joyce's *Finnegans Wake*; Conrad's *Heart of Darkness*; Dalgliesh's *The Silver Pencil*

Emotional Content:

Why has "Daddy" been embraced for half a century as an angry poem? Where in "Daddy" is Plath's language playful? What other feelings are there?

Structure:

Sylvia Plath's "Daddy" is constructed in sixteen five-line stanzas. A five-line stanza is called a *quintet*. The number five, in the tarot and Qabalah, is a number of conflict, fighting, and competition. Where do you see this reflected, intentionally or coincidentally, in Plath's poem?

Discuss Plath's line breaks, and why you believe she might have ended a line with a certain word, enjambed with the next line. What effect does this create? What if you changed Plath's enjambment? Would the poem still be successful?

What if Plath had written "Daddy" as a prose poem with no lines at all? Would the meaning have still come across for you? Why or why not?

Diagram the rhyme scheme in "Daddy," which begins a/a/b/c/a in the first stanza. Do certain sounds call your attention? How so? Where and what are the repeating words and sounds? Are there rhymes? Variations of rhyme? Near-rhyme? Slant rhymes? Assonance?

Discussion Questions:

Traditional Classrooms: Instructor might ask some or all of these questions aloud, write them on a board, or pass them out in printed quizzes.

Online classes: It is advised to post a separate discussion thread for each question. The Instructor should start the thread with an explanatory title, and then post the question in the body of the posting. A related graphic can help the student make the associations explained in *Decoding Sylvia Plath's "Daddy."* Search the Web and use graphics you deem appropriate, respecting copyright law and any necessary permissions.

Suggested graphics can be found on:

http://www.pinterest.com/juliagordonbramer.

1. Connecting the Plath poem "The Rival" to "Daddy": How do these words work the same or different between Plath's "Daddy" and the earlier poem, "The Rival"? How do themes of Africa and villagers show up in both poems? What about *mausoleum* and *marble*; abasing subjects and standing at a blackboard; stone and a statue? What similar feelings do both poems share?

2. Connecting the Plath poem "Daddy" to "You're": How do these words work alike or differently between Plath's "Daddy" and the next poem, "You're"? How do themes of travel and being unable to speak present in both poems? Discuss the playful rhythms and similarities between Plath's phrases "do not do" and "dodo's mode."

3. What is the point of view of this poem and where is the irony in Plath calling "Daddy" a "bastard"? *[Students should define the word "bastard" and consider the narrator's situation in the poem]*

4. At the time Plath wrote "Daddy," she had two young children and read and reviewed many children's books. Despite the subject matter, does "Daddy" also remind you of a children's book? How so? *[rhythm, rhyme, and meter]*

5. Knowing what you now do about Jews and gypsies, do you feel Plath had a right to align herself with these groups of people? Why or why not?

6. In what lines/parts of Plath's "Daddy" do you see references to the mythological queens pictured in the tarot?

7. The related subjects of Brutus, Britain, and British royalty are woven throughout the poem "Daddy." Identify where they each show up in the poem and explain.

8. In what lines/parts of Plath's "Daddy" do you see references to Sigmund Freud? With Freud in mind, how is the poem's final word, *through*, important?

9. The planet Saturn and its alchemical element of lead are a theme of Plath's "Daddy." Identify where they show up in the poem and explain.

10. Summarize how Shakespeare, Joyce, Conrad and Dalgliesh's works appear in Plath's "Daddy."

Activities for Exploration

Students can individually report on themes, being assigned the responsibility to inform the group, for example, as to who Clytemnestra was, to explain or diagram the constellation of Sobieski's Shield, or to summarize an influential literary work partly inspiring this poem.

Rewrite Plath's "Daddy," but change the tense to simple past or future. What does the poem look like? Does it still work in meter and rhythm? Do the feeling and meaning still come across?

Visually diagram key thematic connections (mirrors) in "Daddy" with a mind-map. Encourage students to get as creative as they want, either drawing by hand or using the computer. Look online for examples or models of mind-maps.

Creative Writing Workshop Activities

Re-read the first Tarot/Qabalah mirror for "Daddy," and then study the cards of the queens in the tarot's minor arcana. You can choose actually to meditate, free-write, or explore other occult practices if you like, making the queens your primary focus. Does one queen, in particular, speak to you? Record first impressions, lines channeled to you, or ideas. Like Plath's poem, your words do not have to reveal an immediate, obvious connection with the queens. Perhaps only you will understand how your words relate or stemmed from this exercise.

Develop these ideas into a poem or short story, as appropriate to your class and classroom time, and be prepared to present to the group if requested to do so.

The *Fixed Stars Govern A Life: Decoding Sylvia Plath* system, in summary:

Every poem in *Ariel* has six mirrors, reflecting the Qabalah's six-sided Tree of Life:

First: Tarot/Qabalah symbolism

Second: Alchemy

Third: Mythology

Fourth: Astronomy & Astrology

Fifth: History & World Events

Sixth: Arts & Humanities

Not only did Plath write one poem containing six perfect and different correspondences within the same set of words, but she did this **forty times** in *Ariel*—all in perfect relation to the tarot/Qabalah.

The poem "Daddy," and all Plath's *Ariel* poems, resonate with readers fifty years later because they include qabalistic subconscious touch-points. Readers don't have to understand it to feel it. It is a kind of a spell.

All facets work together to support the whole, creating enlightenment, paralleling the Qabalah's Tree of Life.

For more information, email: DecodingSylviaPlath@gmail.com.

> "And above all, watch with glittering eyes the whole world around you because the greatest secrets are always hidden in the most unlikely places. Those who don't believe in magic will never find it."
> —Roald Dahl

Bibliography

Abraham, Lyndy. *A Dictionary of Alchemical Imagery.* Cambridge, UK: Cambridge University Press, 1998. Print. p. 106.

Alexander, Paul. *Rough Magic: A Biography of Sylvia Plath.* New York: Da Capo Press, 1999.

Allen, Richard Hinckley. *Star Names: Their Lore and Meaning* reprinted from Dover edition, 1963. Web. 3 October 2010. http://penelope.uchicago.edu/Thayer/E/Gazetteer/Topics/astronomy/_Texts/secondary/ALLSTA/Scutum_Sobiescianum*.html

Blake, William (1757-1827). The Poetical Works. 1908. Selections From Jerusalem. "To The Jews." *Jerusalem,* f. 27 .Web. 18 June 2017. http://www.bartleby.com/235/313.html

Bloom, Harold. *Kabbalah and Criticism.* 1981. New York: Continuum.

Boddy-Evans, Alistair. *"The Lovedu Rain Queen: Rain Rituals in Southern Africa and a Royal Succession Lasting Two Centuries."* Web. 3, October 2010. http://africanhistory.about.com/od/peopl1/a/LoveduRainQueen.htm

Bradbury, Reginald A. "Brutus the Trojan." Courtesy of the Kingdom Voice. Web. 3 October 2010. http://www.ensignmessage.com/archives/Brutus.html

Brutus, Dennis. *Compleate Poems.* Web. 2 July 2017. http://ccs.ukzn.ac.za/files/Dennis%20Compleate-poems.pdf

Conrad, Joseph. *The Heart of Darkness.* Forgotten Books. First published in 1902. Reprinted 2008. Electronic Text Center, University of Virginia Library. Web. 30 March 2011. http://etext.virginia.edu/toc/modeng/public/ConDark.html

Coughlan, Sean. "London's Heart of Stone" for BBC News Magazine. Web. 3 October 2010. http://www.inthemedievalmiddle.com/2006/05/stone-of-brutus.html

Dalgliesh, Alice. *The Silver Pencil*. The Scribner Press, 1944. Designated a Newbery Honor Book. (Plath kept an 11-page hand-stapled booklet entitled "The Treasures of Sylvia Plath" with her notes on book-club reading. This booklet may be found in Plath MSS. V of the Sylvia Plath archives at the Lilly Library, Indiana University-Bloomington.)

Ezakwantu Gallery http://www.ezakwantu.com/Tribes%20-%20Ba%20Lobedu%20-%20Lobedu%20-%20Northern%0Basotho%20-%20Balobedu%20-%20Lovedu.htm.Web. 4 April, 2010.

Freud, Sigmund. "Remembering, Repeating and Working-Through (Further Recommendations On The Technique of Psycho-Analysis II)." 1914. Errinern, Wiederholen und Durcharbeiten (Weitere Ratschläge zur Technik der Psychoanalyse, II). Internationale Zeitschrift für ärztliche Psychoanalyse, 2, 485-491; Remembering, repeating and working-through. SE, 12: 147-156.Web. 18 June 2017. http://www.history.ucsb.edu/faculty/marcuse/classes/201/articles/1914 FreudRemembering.pdf Web. 18 June 2017.

Freud, Sigmund. *Totem and Taboo: Resemblances Between the Psychic Lives of Savages and Neurotics*. 1919. London: George Routledge and Sons, Ltd. Stanford University Libraries. https://www.stmarys-ca.edu/sites/default/files/attachments/files/Totem_and_Taboo.pdf. Web. 18 June 2017.

Freud, Sigmund. *A General Introduction to Psychoanalysis*. 1915.https://eduardolbm.files.wordpress.com/2014/10/a-general-introduction-to-psychoanalysis-sigmund-freud.pdf

Geoffrey of Monmouth, *Historia Regum Britanniae* 1.3-18, 2.1 From History of the Kings of Britain/ Book 1. Translation based on Aaron Thompson and J. A. Giles (1842). Web. 3, October 2010. http://en.wikisource.org/wiki/History_of_the_Kings_of_Britain/Book_1#3

Gollancz, Israel (editor). *Wynnere and Wastoure*. Contained in The Parlement of the Thre Ages: An Alliterative Poem of the XIVth Century, Now First Edited, from Manuscripts in the British Museum. London: Nichols and Sons, 1897. With introduction, notes, and appendices containing the poem of "Winnere and Wastoure," and illustrative texts by Israel Gollancz.

Gordon-Bramer. *Fixed Stars Govern a Life: Decoding Sylvia Plath*, Volume One. 2013. Stephen F. Austin State University Press.

Graves, Robert. *The White Goddess: a historical grammar of poetic myth*. 1948. Farrar, Straus and Giroux, New York.

h2g2: The London Stone. http://www.bbc.co.uk/dna/h2g2/A863309 Web. 3 October, 2010.

Harper, Douglas. "root." Online Etymology Dictionary. http://dictionary.reference.com/browse/root Web. 5 October 2010.

Hughes, Gerald. *Ted And I: A Brother's Memoir*. The Robson Press, London. 2012. p 12.

Hughes, Ted. *Birthday Letters*. Farrar, Straus and Giroux. New York. 1998.

Joyce, James. *The Portable James Joyce*. With an introduction and notes by Harry Levin. 1946. The Viking Press. Sylvia Plath's personal annotated copy of this book is held in the Sylvia Plath Archives at the Lilly Library at Indiana University, Bloomington, Indiana.

London "The Tower of London: Instruments of Torture". Web. Last accessed 5 October 2010. http://london.allinfo-about.com/features/torture2.html

Lundstrom, Meg. "A Wink from the Cosmos." Originally published in *Intuition Magazine*, May 1996. Web. http://www.flowpower.com/What%20is%20Synchronicity.htm 26 August, 2016.

Mark. The Gospel According To Mark. The New Testament. King James Version. https://www.biblegateway.com/passage/?search=Mark%2012:13-17;&version=KJV. Web. Last accessed 7 June 2016.

Macmillan, Harold. *Pointing The Way 1959–1961*, London: Macmillan, 1972.

Meyers, Lucas. *Crow Steered Bergs Appeared: A Memoir of Ted Hughes and Sylvia Plath*. Sewanee, Tennessee: Proctor's Hall Press. 2001. Print.

Palmer, Alan. *The Decline and Fall of the Ottoman Empire,* New York: M. Evans and Company. 1992.

Plath, Sylvia. *Ariel: The Restored Edition*. Foreword by Frieda Hughes. New York: HarperPerennial. 2004. pp. 74-76. Print.

Plath, Sylvia. *The Collected Poems*. Ed. by Ted Hughes. 2008. New York: Harper Perennial Modern Classics. Print.

Plath, Sylvia. *The Unabridged Journals of Sylvia Plath*. Ed. by Karen V. Kukil. New York: Anchor Books, 2000. Print.

Rákóczi, Basil Ivan. *The Painted Caravan: a penetration into the secrets of the tarot cards.* 1954, L.J.C. Boucher, The Hague. Print.

Rhodes James, Robert. *A Spirit Undaunted: The Political Role of George VI*, London: Little, Brown and Co. 1998. Print.

Radin, Paul (Editor). *African Folktales*. New York: Schocken Books. 1952. Print.

Roob, Alexander. *The Hermetic Cabinet: Alchemy & Mysticism*. New York: Taschen. 2009. Print.

Sedler, M.J. "Freud's Concept of Working Through." Psychoanalytic Quarterly. 1983. Jan; 52(1):73-98. NCBI PubMed. Web. 18 June 2017. https://www.ncbi.nlm.nih.gov/pubmed/6836082

Sharman-Burke, Juliet and Liz Greene. *The Mythic Tarot*. New York: Simon and Schuster. 1986. Print.

Shakespeare, William. *Julius Caesar*.

Shakespeare, William. *Henry VI*, part 2, Act IV, Scene VI.

Stevenson, Anne. *Bitter Fame: A Life of Sylvia Plath*. New York: Penguin Books.1998. Print.

Voices and Visions. "Sylvia Plath" Directed and Produced by Lawrence Pitkethly. © Annenberg Foundation. Film. 1988.

Specific References by Section:

About the Poem "Daddy"

"…spoken by a girl" (*Ariel*, 196)

Discovering the Connections

Jung's synchronicity and the *acausal connecting principle*; photon experiments (Lundstrom)

"Daddy" and its Position in the Minor Arcana of the Tarot

Rákóczi quote (Rákóczi, 70)
"Dialogue Over A Ouija Board" (CP, 276-286)

A Little About Qabalah

Harold Bloom quote on *mirrors*, (Bloom, 12)

Ich, Ich, Ich, I am I

"…*Aziluth, Beriah, Yezirah*, and *Assiya*" (Roob, 27)

The Black Consciousness of Ego

"Getting There" (*Ariel*, 57-59)

On Being Thirty

"Thirty years now I have labored" (*CP,* 129)

Second Mirror: Alchemy

"…father and daughter, and king and son" (Abraham, 106)

Meet Omphale/Thetis/Medea

"…Pan the Devil" (Sharman-Burke)
"…reigning for seven years each" (Graves, 128)
"…sea-beast king/father Poseidon" (Graves, 360)
"…system into a patriarchal one" (Graves, 390)

Telamon's Off at the Root

"…Talus, who is equated with Achilles" (Graves, 303)
"…he that dares to suffer" (Graves, 136-138)

Plath's Evocation of History in "Daddy"

"…he evoked the past to illuminate the present" (Joyce, 14)
"…his mother embodies religion" (Joyce, 7)
"…legend of the founding of Britain by King Brutus" (Gollancz)
"Appointed Place for My People Israel" (Bradbury)

The Stone's Connection to Jews and William Blake

"…all forms of horrible screws employed in the Tower…" (London)
General history of London Stone (H2G2)

Brutus's London Stone

"…King of Britain was said to have first stepped" (Geoffrey)

Jewish Connections and William Blake

"To the Jews" (Blake)

The Brutal Tax Collector

"Render therefore unto Caesar…" (Mark 12:17)
"…Master of Horse for William the Conqueror" (G. Hughes, 12)
"Doomsday" (*CP*, 316)

Other British Kings

"…South African bodyguards as "The Gestapo" (Rhodes, 294)
"…the heart and stomach of a man" (Macmillan, 466-472)

Apartheid in "Daddy"

"…Plath's best female friends in Cambridge" (Stevenson, 101)
"…African students suffering through Apartheid" (Journals, 380)
"…South Africa's The Daily News, 25 March 2009" (Brutus)

The Rain Queen

"…a terrible husband by her king father" (Radin, 56-59)
"…ruling until 1980" (Boddy)
"…men are not able to inherit the throne" (Ezakwantu)

Polish Connections

History of the Ottoman Empire (Palmer)

Sigmund Freud, Father of Psychoanalysis

"Remembering, Repeating and Working-Through" (Freud)
"…through a will to remember" (Sedler)
"the daddy inside of her, *not* her beloved father" (Voices)

"I'll never speak to God again…" (Alexander, 32)
"…draining the ego" (Journals, 447)
"…swastika represents 'The fullest extent of sovereignty" (Graves, 410)
"…adopted by the Nazis, unlucky" (Graves, 445)
"…sounding 'Freudian' in her journals" (*Journals*, 92, 98)
"…she wrote of actually reading Freud" (*Journals*, 306)

Fifth Mirror: Astrology and Astronomy

"…Hughes' goal to awaken this sleeping gift" (Myers, 9)

Sobieski's Shield and Other Stars

"…the tail of the Serpent and the head of Sagittarius" (Allen)

Hail, Caesar!

Shakespeare quotation from William Shakespeare's *Julius Caesar*, Act 1, Scene 2, 140-141

The Freudian *Finnegans Wake*

"…my cold mad feary father" (*Journals*, 381)

Daddy's *Heart of Darkness*

"…Voices, voices—" (Conrad, 64)

The Silver Pencil

"I don't love God." (Dalgliesh, 34)
"I'm *through*." (Dalgliesh, 138)
"'Through? / Gee baby, you are rare'" (*Ariel*, 39).

What Students Are Saying About the *Fixed Stars Govern a Life: Decoding Sylvia Plath* System:

"What I learned was that she [Sylvia Plath] fooled everyone. Her work is infinitely more complicated than people think; it's hardly about her life at all. She wrote some kind of double metaphor, building stories within stories that only the most discerning of readers would be able to determine. Plath didn't write Hemingway's metaphorical glaciers, she made Russian nesting dolls." C.A.

"I feel that I have at last met the Master Gypsy. In *Fixed Stars Govern a Life: Decoding Sylvia Plath*, by Julia Gordon-Bramer, whole new esoteric references were opened up to me. Here is a method of scholarship and a way of looking at poetry that has never before been accomplished with such depth. In poetry we read the poet and study them where they are found *in situ*, but not to this extent. Here was global learning at its best. It was not easy. There were many references that I had to research, and yet it brought my understanding to a higher level. I felt as if I had always just looked at the surface of poetry—not deep enough. As a writer of poetry it resonated with me because within my mind I could see that I pulled references when writing from the same sources as was quoted in this book. When I write consciously or subconsciously, as pointed out in *Fixed Stars Govern a Life*, I myself am drawing from my own time, my own place, historic events, my library, the things I knew, felt and studied just as Plath was." T.S.

"I became a little bit frightened, to tell you the truth. I would lie awake at night thinking about it, how connected we are and how deep everything goes. I felt like Plath in "Elm": 'I am incapable of more knowledge.' This class got in my head and I began to see the mystical patterns in everything." E.A.

"No one cares more about Sylvia Plath's works [than Gordon-Bramer]. With every assignment, there is an overview of the poem to read that week, writing tips, history and context, and of course …mysticism. It was these things that made this class easy to fall in love with. We were guided along the entire time." T.D.

"I stepped into the class on the recommendation from a friend who took the course last semester. She said that your writing, exploring Plath's writing, and the nature of the in-depth discussions would change my life. She was right. [...] This class gave me courage and the belief in my words." D.M.

"This class was designed by one of Lindenwood's best instructors, and one of the best Plath scholars anywhere, in my opinion. I feel truly honored to have learned from her. She raises the bar to a whole new level, and inspires me to be better as a writer and reader. Excellent." W.M.

"These classes are responsible for a paradigm shift in how I look at the world, and I feel that is a gift." M.D.

"Julia Gordon-Bramer does a phenomenal job of breaking down the material and providing thought provoking discussion. As someone with minimal background in poetry, I feel confident going forward as I've learned to delve deep into the multi-layers and meanings that are present." D.G.

"It is clear that these poems are not just confessional poems. The imagery is so universal. I often found [Plath's] references in the mirrors about universal topics of war, freedom, prejudice, entrapment, infidelity, searching, truth, love and human growth and self-actualization. These topics are just as vital today as they were when she wrote them in the early sixties." T.C.

ABOUT THE AUTHOR

Julia Gordon-Bramer has been a tarot reader for nearly forty years, almost ten professionally. She received her bachelor's degree in literature and language from Webster University in St. Louis, and her MFA in creative writing (poetry and fiction) from the University of Missouri-St. Louis. While always "a Plathie," she began her serious scholarship in 2007, going farther and farther down the rabbit hole of mysticism, from which there appears to be no return. She teaches on Plath and other subjects in the Lindenwood University graduate-level creative writing program and has presented on Plath at universities and libraries across America and in the United Kingdom. In 2013, *The Riverfront Times* voted her St. Louis' Best Local Poet. In addition to *Decoding Sylvia Plath's "Daddy,"* she is author of *Fixed Stars Govern a Life: Decoding Sylvia Plath* (2014, Stephen F. Austin State University Press) and the forthcoming *Decoding* books (Magi Press), as well as *The Magician's Girl*, a biography of the mysticism of Sylvia Plath and Ted Hughes. It is Julia Gordon-Bramer's greatest wish to show the world that we haven't even scratched the surface of understanding Plath's creative genius, and more importantly, that there is something bigger going on which pulls the strings of everything.

Please give this book a review on Amazon, Goodreads, or other sites, and visit www.juliagordonbramer.com and www.magipress.co, or write DecodingSylviaPlath@gmail.com for more information.

www.ingramcontent.com/pod-product-compliance
Lightning Source LLC
Chambersburg PA
CBHW070542300426
44113CB00011B/1759